START READING

A Basic Reader in English

FRANKLIN I. BACHELLER

Intensive English Language Institute
Utah State University, Logan, Utah

Prentice Hall Regents, Englewood Cliffs, New Jersey 07632

Library of Congress Cataloging-in-Publication Data

Bacheller, Franklin I.
   Start reading : a basic reader in English / Franklin I. Bacheller
; illustrated by Xandy Schultz.

   ISBN 0-13-753724-7
   1. English language—Textbooks for foreign speakers.
2. Readers—1950–   I. Title.
PE1128.B22   1991
428.6'4—dc20   90-31663
                                                        CIP

Editorial/production supervision and
   interior design: **Kala Dwarakanath**
Cover design: **Photo Plus Art**
Pre-Press buyer: **Ray Keating**
Manufacturing buyer: **Lori Bulwin**

Illustrations: **Xandy Schultz**

© 1991 by Prentice-Hall, Inc.
A Division of Simon & Schuster
Englewood Cliffs, New Jersey 07632

Printed in the United States of America
10 9 8 7 6 5 4 3

ISBN   0-13-753724-7

Prentice-Hall International (UK) Limited, *London*
Prentice-Hall of Australia Pty. Limited, *Sydney*
Prentice-Hall Canada Inc., *Toronto*
Prentice-Hall Hispanoamericana, S.A., *Mexico*
Prentice-Hall of India Private Limited, *New Delhi*
Prentice-Hall of Japan, Inc., *Tokyo*
Simon & Schuster Asia Pte. Ltd., *Singapore*
Editora Prentice-Hall do Brasil, Ltda., *Rio de Janeiro*

I would like to thank Susan Carkin, Lee Ann Rawley and the rest of the staff of the Intensive English Language Institute, Utah State University, for their support and encouragement. I also appreciate the assistance of Gene Pleisch, Susan Sojka and Maria Wilson in piloting the text in their classrooms.

Thanks also go to Xandy Schultz for her illustrations and to reviewers whose comments and suggestions helped improve this book.

Contents

Preface

Start Reading is for beginning to high-beginning students of English as a Second or Foreign Language. Throughout the book students read charts, narratives, stories, and expository passages. Then they do exercises that help them to learn to:

* recognize words and phrases
* recognize main ideas
* guess meanings of words
* answer questions by inferring from context of readings
* recall, summarize and discuss readings
* solve problems presented by readings.

      Start Reading is an integrative text. The exercises focus on the content of the readings and require students to apply all four skills of listening, speaking, reading, and writing.

Students

This text is for students whose overall English proficiency approximates that of students found typically in the beginning level of most academic ESL programs. These students have studied English previously, perhaps while in high school, but they can understand, speak, read, and write only simple English. Many still translate to and from their native language in their attempts to communicate; they rely heavily on bilingual dictionairies when reading.

Organization

Start Reading has 10 lessons, which provide enough material for 40 to 60 hours of classroom study.

      Each lesson is divided into four parts. The first three contain listening activities, readings (charts, narratives, short stories, or expository passages), and various skill building exercises.

      The fourth part consists of suggestions for outside reading to augment the students' reading experience. Students are referred to encyclopedias or other reference books to find specific information (usually numbers and names) relating to the subject matter of the readings.

Exercises

Most exercises have been developed out of the context of readings.

Listening exercises help students develop expectations about the reading. The exercises attempt to do the following:

* stimulate thinking about the topic
* offer an overview of the reading

- provide background and/or additional information
- introduce important vocabulary

Reading comprehension exercises require that students

- find information in the reading
- use the information to solve problems

Reading skill exercises give students practice in word and phrase recognition, reference, skimming, scanning, recognition of main ideas, outlining, and inferring answers from context.

Vocabulary exercises focus on words students must know in order to understand listening and reading passages. For most exercises, students first guess the meanings of words from the context of a reading or a listening. Then they fill in blanks in short paragraphs with vocabulary items. Often, the paragraphs summarize the reading or listening.

Other vocabulary exercises focus on synonyms and antonyms; prefixes and suffixes; and grammatical forms.

Instructor's Manual

An instructor's manual accompanies this text and contains the following:

- scripts for listening exercises (prereading exercises)
- for each reading, one or more suggestions for activities to invoke the students' background knowledge of the subject
- suggested procedures for various exercises
- answers to exercises
- suggestions for additional outside readings, which may supplement or replace the readings suggested in the fourth part of each lesson.

Topics

The readings in each lesson focus on closely related topics. In the first lesson, for example, all three readings are concerned with some aspect of air travel (Major Developments in Transport Aircraft, Alone on a 747, and Flying Through Time Zones).

Moreover, all readings and charts in the text center around the eight topics shown below. Topics with which students are familiar tend to occur earlier in the text than those in which students may lack familiarity.

Physical World	**Lesson**
Flying through Time Zones	1
Air Distances from Honolulu	2
Longitude and Latitude	3
World Climates	3
Solar System	5

Technology

Theoretical Base

The following materials support many of the techniques employed in **Start Reading**.

For support of language instruction based on practice and language use rather than formal instruction: Karl J. Krahnke and Mary Ann Cristison *Recent Language Research and Some Language Teaching Principles*. 1983. TESOL Quarterly, 17,4.

Short stories and narratives: John W. Oller, Jr. *Story Writing Principles and ESL Teaching*. 1983. TESOL Quarterly, 17,1.

Simplified versions to introduce readings: Ulla Connor. *Recall of Text: Differences Between First and Second Language Readers*. 1984. TESOL Quarterly, 18,2.

Topics familiar to the reader: Patricia L. Carrell and Joan C. Eisterhold. *Schema Theory and ESL Reading Pedagogy*. 1983. TESOL Quarterly, 17,4.

Exercises to invoke the reader's background knowledge . . . Use of authentic reading materials: June Phillips. *Reading in the ESL and Foreign Language Classroom*. A workshop presented at Utah State University, Logan, Utah, 1989.

Combining receptive and productive skills: Ruth Spack. *Literature, Reading, Writing, and ESL: Bridging the Gaps*. TESOL Quarterly, 19,4.

Speaking and writing exercises based on reading materials: Giuseppina Cortese. *From Receptive to Productive in Post-Intermediate EFL Classes: A Pedagogical Experiment*. 1985. TESOL Quarterly, 19,1.

Lesson 1

BOEING 747	
Seating capacity	Speed (miles per hour)
447–490	610

CONCORDE	
Seating capacity	Speed (miles per hour)
132	1350

Part One — **AIRCRAFT**

Listening

Listen for the main idea.

Your teacher will give you some information. Listen to the information. Then answer the following question.

What is the information about? (Circle the letter in front of the correct answer.)

a. airplanes

b. people

Listen for words.

Fill in the blanks while listening to the information again. Use the following words and expressions.

> faster   larger
> few   miles per hour
>   passengers

Airplanes are _____ and _____
today. Early airplanes carried only a _____ people. They
traveled about 100 _____. Today, some airplanes carry
more than 400 _____ and fly more than 500 _____
_____.

Guess the meanings of words.

*Read the information. Then read the statements following the information. Put **T** in front of statements that are true. Put **F** in front of statements that are false.*

Some airplanes fly 300 miles per hour. They can go 300 miles in one
hour.

_____   1.   *Miles per hour* tells how fast something goes.
_____   2.   *Miles per hour* tells how big something is.

A Douglas DC-10 can fly 620 miles per hour. A Boeing 707 can fly 578
miles per hour.

_____   3.   A Boeing 707 is faster than a Douglas DC-10.
_____   4.   A Douglas DC-10 is faster than a Boeing 707.

A Douglas DC-10 can carry 252 people. A Boeing 707 can carry 135
people.

_____   5.   A Boeing 707 is larger than a Douglas DC-10.
_____   6.   A Douglas DC-10 is larger than a Boeing 707.

Early airplanes did not carry many people. They carried only a few
people. For example, the Junkers Ju52 carried only 17 passengers. Today,
airplanes carry many passengers. For example, the Boeing 747 can carry 490
passengers.

_____   7.   *Few* means "not many."
_____   8.   *Few* means "many."
_____   9.   Passengers are people who ride on airplanes.

Use words in context.

Write one word or expression in each blank.

faster   few   larger   miles per hour   passengers

Airplanes are _____ today. Early airplanes carried only a _____ _____. Airplanes are also _____ today. They can now fly more than 500 _____ _____.

Check your comprehension.

Your teacher will tell you the information again. Answer the following questions while listening. Circle the letter in front of the correct answer.

1. Did early airplanes carry many passengers?
   a. yes
   b. no

2. How fast did they fly?
   a. 100 miles per hour
   b. 300 miles per hour
   c. 500 miles per hour

3. How many passengers do some airplanes carry today?
   a. 100
   b. 400
   c. 300

4. How fast do airplanes fly today?
   a. 100 miles per hour
   b. 300 miles per hour
   c. 500 miles per hour

Listen to the information again. Check your answers while you listen.

Reading

Preview the reading.

Look at the chart. Then answer the following question.

Is the chart about aircraft?

a. yes

b. no

TRANSPORT AIRCRAFT (1915–1974)*

PROPELLER AIRCRAFT

Year	Name	Number of Passengers	Speed (Miles per hour)
1915	Junkers F13	4	87
1922	Handley Page W.8b	12–14	90
1926	Ford 4AT Trimotor	10–11	107
1928	Fokker FVIIb-3m	10	111
1928	Boeing Model 80A	18	125
1932	Junkers Ju52	17	152
1933	Boeing 247	10	189
1935	Douglas DC-3	21	192
1940	Boeing SA-307B Stratoliner	33	222
1942	Douglas DC-4	44–86	227
1946	Douglas DC-6	52	310
1946	Lockheed Constellation	44–81	327
1947	Boeing 377 Stratocruiser	55–117	327

JET AIRCRAFT

Year	Name	Passengers	Speed
1952	Comet I	36	450
1958	Boeing 707	135	578
1959	Douglas DC-8	116–176	544
1970	Boeing 747	447–490	610
1971	Douglas DC-10	252	620

SUPERSONIC AIRCRAFT

Year	Name	Passengers	Speed
1973	Concorde	132	1,350

---

*Examples only. This chart does not list every kind of airplane.

Find specific information.

Answer the following questions based on information from the preceding chart.

1. The chart lists three kinds of aircraft. What are they?
   a. propeller aircraft
   b. _____ _____
   c. _____

2. How many examples does the chart give of each kind of aircraft?
   a. propeller aircraft   (13)
   b. _____   ( )
   c. _____ _____   ( )

3. The chart tells you four things about each aircraft. What are those four things?
   a. year
   b. name

   c. _____
   d. _____

4. Which is the newest aircraft on the chart? Which is the oldest aircraft on the chart?

   _____

5. Look under "Speed." What was the speed of the Junkers F13?

   _____

6. Which aircraft on the chart is the fastest? Which aircraft is the slowest?

   _____

7. Complete the following chart.

Year	Name	Kind of Aircraft	Number of Passengers	Speed (Miles per hour)
1915	Junkers F13	Propeller	4	87
____	Boeing Model 80A	_____	_____	_____
____	Douglas DC-3	_____	_____	_____
____	Boeing 377 Stratocruiser	_____	_____	_____
____	Boeing 707	_____	_____	_____
____	Boeing 747	_____	_____	_____
____	Concorde	_____	_____	_____

Use information to make guesses.

*Study carefully the chart you just completed. Then put **T** (true) in front of three statements that you think are true. Put **F** (false) in front of the other statement.*

_____ 1. Airplanes are larger today.

_____ 2. Propeller planes are larger and faster than jet planes.

_____ 3. Early airplanes were slower.

_____ 4. Jet planes are newer than propeller planes.

Make and use new words.

Write one word in each blank.

ADJECTIVE	COMPARATIVE	SUPERLATIVE
new	newer	newest
old	_____	_____
large	_____	_____
small	_____	_____
fast	_____	_____

Read the following information about Douglas aircraft.

The Douglas DC-3 began service in 1936.
The Douglas DC-6 began service in 1946.
The Douglas DC-10 began service in 1971.

Fill in the blanks with the following words.

newer   newest   older   oldest

The DC-3 is the _____*oldest*_____ of the three aircraft. The DC-6 is _____ than the DC-3, but it is _____ _____ than the DC-10. The DC-10 is the _____.

Recall the information.

Try to answer the following questions without looking back at the chart.

1. How many different kinds of aircraft are listed in the chart?
2. What is the name of the fastest airplane?
3. What is the name of the slowest airplane?
4. What is the name of the smallest airplane?
5. What is the name of the largest airplane?

Part Two — JUAN

Listening

Listen for the main idea.

Your teacher will tell you a story. Listen to the story. Then answer the following question.

What is the story about? (Circle the letter in front of the correct answer.)
a. going to a new country to go to school
b. going to a new university in your country

Listen for words.

Fill in the blanks while listening to the story again. Use the following words and expressions.

airplane	thinking about
foreign country	traveling
	worried about

    Juan is on an _____. He is _____ to a _____. He is going to go to school there. He is _____ his family. He is also _____ his life in the new country and about going to the university there. He must learn more English before he can take university classes. He is _____ learning English.

Guess the meanings of words.

*Read the information. Then read the statements following the information. Put **T** in front of statements that are true. Put **F** in front of statements that are false.*

A foreign country is not your country. It is a different country.

_____   1. Juan is from Peru. To Juan, the United States is a foreign country.

_____   2. Juan is from Peru. To Juan, Peru is a foreign country.

Juan must learn English before he can go to the university. He knows only a little English now. He thinks it will be difficult to learn English. He is worried about learning English.

_____   3. When Juan worries about learning English, he feels bad.

_____   4. When Juan worries about learning English, he feels very good.

Use words in context.

Write one word or expression in each blank.

airplane   foreign country   worried about

Juan is on an _____. He is traveling to a _____. He doesn't know much English, so he is _____ _____ learning enough English to study at the university.

Check your comprehension.

Your teacher will tell you the information again. Answer the following questions while listening. Circle the letter in front of the correct answer.

1. Where is Juan?
    a. at the university
    b. on an airplane

2. Where is he going?
    a. to another country
    b. home

3. What is he going to do there?
    a. think about his friends
    b. study

4. Is he thinking about his family?

    a. yes

    b. no

5. Is he worried about learning English?

    a. yes

    b. no

Listen to the story again. Check your answers while you listen.

Reading

Preview the reading.

Look at the reading. Then answer the following questions.

1. Is someone on a Boeing 747?

    a. yes

    b. no

2. Is this person going to go to school in another country?

    a. yes
    b. no

3. Is this person happy?

    a. yes
    b. no

4. Is this person worried?

    a. yes
    b. no

Alone on a 747

Here I am—alone on this Boeing 747. I am going to another country to go to school. I am happy and excited. But I am also lonely. My family and my friends are at home. I am up here in the sky, halfway over an ocean.

I am not afraid, but I am worried. What will my new life be like? Where will I live? Will people be friendly? Will I learn enough English to go to school? Will someone meet me at the airport?

Four hours ago, I was at the airport in my country. My family and friends were with me. Everyone was saying, "Good-bye, Juan. Good luck!"

I looked at my parents' faces. I saw big smiles. I knew that they were proud of me. But I also saw tears in their eyes. I knew that they were going to miss me.

At home it is two o'clock in the afternoon. My family is learning to live without me. And now I must learn to live without them.

My parents want me to go to school. I want to go to school. So here I am on this airplane.

I must stop thinking about my family and friends. I will be in a new country in three hours. I must be brave because I will have a lot to do.

Check your comprehension.

Read the story about Juan again. Answer the questions that follow each section of the story.

Here I am—alone on this Boeing 747. I am going to another country to go to school. I am happy and excited. But I am also lonely. My family and my friends are at home. I am up here in the sky, halfway over an ocean.

I am not afraid, but I am worried. What will my new life be like? Where will I live? Will people be friendly? Will I learn enough English to go to school? Will someone meet me at the airport?

At home it is two o'clock in the afternoon. My family is learning to live without me. And now I must learn to live without them.

1. Where is Juan?

   a. in his country
   b. on an airplane
   c. in a foreign country

2. Where are his family and friends?

   a. in his country
   b. in a foreign country

3. Tell how Juan feels:

   Is he happy?   a. yes   b. no
   Is he excited?   a. yes   b. no
   Is he lonely?   a. yes   b. no
   Is he afraid?   a. yes   b. no
   Is he worried?   a. yes   b. no

4. What is Juan worried about:

   His new life?   a. yes   b. no
   Where he will live?   a. yes   b. no
   Flying over an ocean?   a. yes   b. no
   If people will be friendly?   a. yes   b. no
   His family and friends?   a. yes   b. no
   If he will learn enough English?   a. yes   b. no
   If someone will meet him at the airport?   a. yes   b. no

Four hours ago, I was at the airport in my country. My family and friends were with me. Everyone was saying, "Good-bye, Juan. Good luck!"

5. Who was at the airport with Juan?

   a. I
   b. family and friends

I looked at my parents' faces. I saw big smiles. I knew that they were proud of me. But I also saw tears in their eyes. I knew that they were going to miss me.

6. Were Juan's parents proud of him?

   a. yes
   b. no

7. Were his parents also sad?

   a. yes
   b. no

At home it is two o'clock in the afternoon. My family is learning to live without me. And now I must learn to live without them.

My parents want me to go to school. I want to go to school. So here I am on this airplane.

8. Must Juan learn to live alone?

   a. yes
   b. no

9. Do Juan's parents want him to go to school?

   a. yes
   b. no

10. Does Juan want to go to school?

   a. yes
   b. no

Four hours ago, I was at the airport. . . . I will be in a new country in three hours. . . .

11. How long is Juan's flight?

   a. four hours
   b. three hours
   c. seven hours

I must stop thinking about my family and friends. I will be in a new country in three hours. I must be brave because I will have a lot to do.

12. Will Juan be all right in the new country?

   a. maybe
   b. no

Use information to make guesses.

Which sentences from the reading help you guess that Juan is on an airplane? Choose five answers.

a. Here I am—alone on this Boeing 747.

b. I am going to another country.

c. I am up here in the sky.

d. Will someone meet me at the airport?

e. I am happy and excited.

f. Four hours ago, I was at the airport in my country.

Find words with the same or opposite meanings.

Fill in the blanks with one of the following words or expressions.

a lot to do   good-bye
ago   happy
alone   parents

Opposite Meaning

1. I am with someone.   I am _____.
2. I am sad.   I am _____.
3. in four hours   four hours _____.
4. hello   _____

Same Meaning

5. mother and father   _____ _____
6. much to do   _____

Determine the meanings of pronouns.

Read the information. Then circle the answer that has the same meaning as the word just before the parenthesis.

Example—John has a book. It (a. John b. book) is a history book.

Which word has the same meaning as *it—John* or *book*? In this sentence, *it* means "book." So you should choose answer b.

Four hours ago, I was at the airport in my country. My family and friends were with me. Everyone (a. Juan b. family and friends) was saying, "Good-bye, Juan. Good luck!"

I looked at my parents' faces. I saw big smiles. I knew that they (a. parents b. friends) were proud of me. But I also saw tears in their (a. parents' b. friends') eyes. I knew that they (a. parents b. friends) were going to miss me.

At home it is two o'clock in the afternoon. My family is learning to live without me. And now I must learn to live without them (a. family b. friends).

Summarize the reading.

Fill in the blanks with the following words and expressions.

another country   school
family   worried
misses

Juan is going to _____. He is going to go to
_____ there. He is happy and excited, but he is also
_____.

On the airplane, Juan is thinking about his _____
and friends. He _____ them, but he knows that he must
learn to live without them.

Discuss an airplane trip.

Ask someone in your class about an airplane trip she or he has taken.

1. What kind of airplane did you fly on?
2. Where did you go?
3. Why did you go there?
4. Did you go with someone, or did you go alone?
5. How did you feel?

Part Three — FLYING THROUGH
TIME ZONES

Listening

Listen for the main idea.

*Your teacher will give you some information. Listen to the information.
Then answer the following question.*

What is the information about? (Circle the letter in front of the correct answer.)
a. flying in airplanes
b. flying through time zones

Listen for words.

*Fill in the blanks while listening to the information again. Use the
following words and expressions.*

east	loses
gains	time zone
goes through	west

When an airplane flies _____ or _____
_____ for a long distance, it _____ time zones. If it
is flying _____, it _____ one hour for
each _____ it _____. If it is flying
_____, it _____ one hour for each time
zone it _____.

Guess the meanings of words.

*Read the information. Then read the statements following the information. Put **T** in front of statements that are true. Put **F** in front of statements that are false.*

The earth is divided into twenty-four time zones. Time changes by one hour when you go from one time zone to another.

_____   1. If I leave one time zone and enter the next time zone, time will change by one hour.

_____   2. If I leave one time zone and enter the next time zone, time will change by two hours.

It is nine o'clock. You travel west into the next time zone. The time there is eight o'clock. You gain one hour. Your day will now be 25 hours long.

_____   3. You have less time if you gain time.

_____   4. You have more time if you gain time.

It is nine o'clock. You travel east into the next time zone. The time there is ten o'clock. You lose one hour. Your day will now be only 23 hours long.

_____   5. You have less time if you lose time.

_____   6. You have more time if you lose time.

You do the following when you go through a time zone: You enter it, then you travel across it, and then you enter the next time zone.

_____   7. When you "go through" something, you go in and out.

_____   8. When you "go through" something, you just go in. You do not come out.

Use words in context.

Write one word or expression in each blank.

gain or lose   go through   time zones

Airplanes go through _____ when they travel east or west. They _____ one hour for each time zone they _____.

Review directions.

Write one word in each blank.

north	northeast	northwest
south	southeast	southwest
east	west	

Directions

Check your comprehension.

Your teacher will ask you the following questions. Answer by circling the letter in front of the correct answer.

1. Does an airplane go through time zones when it flies east or west?
   a. yes
   b. no

2. Does the time change for each time zone an airplane goes through?
   a. yes
   b. no

3. Does an airplane gain time if it is flying west?
   a. yes
   b. no

4. Does an airplane gain time if it is flying east?
   a. yes
   b. no

Listen to the information again. Check your answers while you listen.

Reading

Preview the reading.

Look at the reading. Then answer the following questions.

1. Is the reading about flying through time zones?
   a. yes
   b. no

2. Does the reading say that an airplane gains or loses time when it travels through time zones?
   a. yes
   b. no

Flying through Time Zones

When an airplane flies east or west for a long distance, it goes through time zones. If the plane is traveling from west to east, it loses one hour for each time zone it goes through. If it is traveling from east to west, it gains one hour for each time zone.

An airplane flying from New York to Los Angeles, passes through three time zones. Los Angeles is west of New York, so the airplane gains three hours.

Underline key phrases.

The following are important phrases from the reading. Look back at the reading. Find these phrases, and underline them.

airplane flies east or west . . .   east to west . . .
goes through time zones . . .   gains one hour . . .
traveling from west to east . . .   for each time zone . . .
loses one hour . . .
for each time zone . . .

Use the reading to solve problems.

Answer the following questions.

1. An airplane flies from Los Angeles to New York.
   a. How many time zones does it go through?
   b. Does it gain time or lose time?
   c. How many hours does it gain or lose?

2. An airplane leaves New York at 7 A.M. and flies to Los Angeles. The flight time is six hours.

   a. How many hours does it take the plane to fly between the two cities?

   b. When the airplane leaves New York, what time is it in Los Angeles?

   c. When the plane arrives in Los Angeles, what time is it in Los Angeles? What time is it in New York?

   d. Does the airplane gain time or lose time?

   e. How many hours does it gain or lose?

   f. How many time zones does the plane go through?

Discuss air flights.

Talk about flights that you have taken.

1. What cities did you travel between?

2. What was the flight time?

3. Did you gain or lose time?

4. How much time?

Part Four

Outside Reading

Learn about a big plane.

Look up Howard Hughes *(look under* Hughes*) in an encyclopedia. Then answer the following questions.*

1. Mr. Hughes built a very large airplane. What was the name of the airplane?

2. When did he build that airplane?

3. Did that airplane ever fly?

Learn about another plane.

Find information about an airplane that is not listed on the chart in Part One of this lesson. Ask your reference librarian to help you find a book that has pictures and short descriptions of airplanes.

Lesson 2

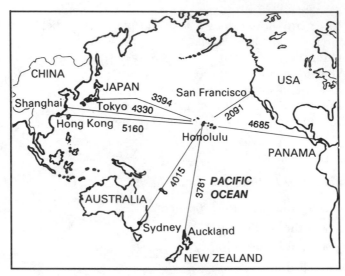

Distances are in nautical miles.

Part One — **AIR DISTANCES**
FROM HONOLULU

Listening

Listen for the main idea.

Your teacher will give you some information. Listen to the information. Then answer the following question.

What is the information about? (Circle the letter in front of the correct answer.)

a. Hawaii

b. San Francisco

Listen for words.

Fill in the blanks while listening to the information again. Use the following words, numbers, and expressions.

chain of islands	Pacific Ocean	2,000	3,400
largest	part	3,800	

Hawaii is _____ of the United States. It is a

_____ in the _____. Honolulu, the

_____ city in Hawaii, is about _____ miles from San Francisco. It is about _____ miles from Tokyo, Japan, and about _____ miles from Auckland, New Zealand.

Guess the meanings of words.

*Read the information. Then read the statements following the information. Put **T** in front of statements that are true. Put **F** in front of statements that are false.*

The state of Hawaii is a chain of islands. There are five large islands. First there is Kauai, second there is Oahu, next there is Molakai, then there is Maui, and finally there is the island of Hawaii. There are also some smaller islands.

_____ 1. There are several islands in a chain of islands
_____ 2. There is only one island in a chain of islands.
_____ 3. Hawaii is part of Kauai.
_____ 4. Kauai is part of Hawaii.

Use words in context.

Write one word or expression in each blank.

chain   Pacific Ocean   part

Hawaii is _____ of the United States. It is a
_____ of islands in the _____.

Check your comprehension.

Your teacher will tell you the information again. Answer the following questions while listening. Circle the letter in front of the correct answer.

1. Where is Hawaii?
   a. in the Pacific Ocean
   b. in Honolulu

2. About how far is Honolulu from San Francisco?
   a. 3,800 miles
   b. 4,000 miles
   c. 2,000 miles

Listen to the information again. Check your answers while listening.

Reading

Preview the reading.

Look at the map. Then answer the following questions.

1. What does the map show?
   a. Atlantic Ocean
   b. Pacific Ocean

2. Look at the lines between Honolulu, Hawaii, and some other cities in the Pacific region. There are numbers below each line. These lines give the distance in miles* between Honolulu and the other cities. What is the distance between Honolulu and San Francisco?

3. Fill in the following chart. Look at the map to find out the correct distances.

AIR DISTANCES FROM HONOLULU TO OTHER CITIES IN THE PACIFIC

Honolulu	to	Auckland, New Zealand	_____
		Hong Kong	_____
		Panama, Panama	_____
		San Francisco, U.S.	_____
		Shanghai, China	_____
		Sydney, Australia	_____
		Tokyo, Japan	_____

*Distances given on the map are in nautical miles. One nautical mile equals 1.852 kilometers.

Guess the meanings of words.

*Read the information. Then read the statements following the information. Put **T** in front of the statement that is true. Put **F** in front of the statement that is false.*

Some people go through Honolulu when they fly from Los Angeles to Tokyo. Other people do not go through Honolulu. They fly directly from Los Angeles to Tokyo.

Which is a direct route?

_____ 1. from San Francisco to Anchorage to Tokyo

_____ 2. from San Francisco to Tokyo.

Use the information to solve problems.

Look at the preceding air distance chart. Write out answers to the following questions.

1. Which city is the closest to Honolulu?

2. Which city is the farthest from Honolulu?

3. How far is it from Hong Kong to Panama if you go through Honolulu? Solve the problem this way:

   Distance from Hong Kong to Honolulu: _____

   Distance from Honolulu to Panama: +   _____

   Total Distance: _____

4. The distance on a direct route from Tokyo to San Francisco is 4,536 nautical miles. How much farther is it if you go through Honolulu? Solve the problem this way:

   a. Determine the distance from Tokyo to San Francisco through Honolulu.
   b. Subtract the direct route distance.

5. How long will it take an airplane to travel from Auckland to San Francisco if it flies at 500 miles per hour? Solve the problem this way:

   a. Determine the distance from Auckland to San Francisco.
   b. Divide that distance by 500.

Review some words.

Supply the missing forms of the adjectives. Some of the words you need are in the questions in the exercise just above.

large   larger   largest
                             closer
_____   _____   _____
_____   _____   farthest

Fill in the blanks with the correct sign.

+   −   ÷   ×

_____ add   _____ multiply
_____ divide   _____ subtract

Recall the information.

Try to answer the following questions without looking back at the air distance chart.

1. Which of the cities on the chart is the closest to Honolulu?
2. Which of the cities is the farthest from Honolulu?

Part Two — **FIRST NIGHT IN A NEW COUNTRY**

Listening

Listen for the main idea.

Your teacher will tell you a story and then ask you some questions. Listen to the story. Then answer the following question.

What is the story about? (Circle the letter in front of the correct answer.)

a. traveling by airplane

b. going to another country

Listen for words.

Fill in the blanks while listening to the information again. Use the following words and expressions.

everywhere	Japanese
for an hour	narrow
Japan	signs

    Mary went to _____. She arrived in the evening. At the airport, she saw _____ in _____. She heard people speaking _____.

    Two friends met her at the airport. They took her to their apartment. On the way, Mary saw _____ streets. People were _____. Cars, buses, and trains were _____, too.

    The apartment was very small. Mary and her friends talked _____ before they went to bed.

    When Mary woke up the next morning, she heard the "ting, ting, ting" of a wind chime. She saw rain falling over a beautiful garden.

    She felt very good.

Find past tense verbs.

The following verbs are in the present tense. Fill in the blanks with the past tense form of the verbs. You can find the answers in the preceding exercise.

Present Tense	**Past Tense**
arrive	_____
feel	_____
hear	_____
meet	_____
see	_____
talk	_____
take	_____
is	_____
go	_____
are	_____
wake up	_____

Guess the meanings of words.

*Read the information. Then read the statements following the information. Put **T** in front of statements that are true. Put **F** in front of statements that are false.*

People in Japan speak Japanese.

_____ 1. Japan is a country; Japanese is a language.
_____ 2. Japan is a language; Japanese is a country.

Signs are everywhere. In an airport, signs tell us where to find our airplane, where to find our bags, etc. On a road, signs tell us when to stop, how fast to go, when to turn, etc.

_____ 3. Signs tell people things. Signs are in writing or in pictures.
_____ 4. Signs are people. These people tell other people things.
_____ 5. *Everywhere* means "in one place."
_____ 6. *Everywhere* means "in all places."

They drove along a wide street for a while. Soon, they turned onto a narrow street. They drove slowly on this street because it wasn't wide enough for all the cars, small trucks, bicycles, and people.

_____ 7. A narrow street is not wide.

Use words in context.

Fill in the blanks with one of the following words or expressions.

everywhere	Japan	narrow
for an hour	Japanese	signs

1. People in _____ speak _____.
2. Many _____ were in Japanese.
3. The streets are not wide. They are _____.
4. People, cars, buses, and trains were _____.
5. They talked _____ before they went to bed.

Check your comprehension.

Your teacher will ask you the following questions. Circle the letter in front of the correct answer.

1. What country did Mary go to?
   a. United States
   b. Japan

2. What language were people at the airport speaking?
   a. Japanese
   b. English

3. Where did Mary's friends take her?
   a. to the airport
   b. to their apartment

4. What did Mary see on the way?
   a. narrow streets, many people, many cars, buses, and trains
   b. many airports and airplanes

5. What did Mary and her friends do at the apartment?
   a. They went to bed right away.
   b. They talked for an hour.

6. The next morning, Mary heard a wind chime and saw a garden. How did she feel?
   a. good
   b. bad

Listen to the information again. Check your answers while you listen.

Reading

Preview the reading.

Look at the reading. Then answer the following question.

Is the story about Mary?
a. yes
b. no

First Night in a New Country

I remember my first hours in Japan.

My plane arrived in the evening. I waited in my seat until the plane stopped. Then I got up and followed the other passengers off the plane.

Inside the terminal, I saw signs written in Japanese. I heard people speaking Japanese fluently. Even little children, only two or three years old, were speaking Japanese much better than I could. And I had been trying so hard to learn it!

I was excited, but a little lonely and afraid. How happy I was when I heard two American friends who had come to meet me call out, "Mary! Mary! Long time no see!"

My friends took me to their apartment. From the car, I saw a new world. Everything I looked at interested me. I saw streets that were narrow and crowded with people and cars. I saw buses and trains everywhere.

The apartment was very small. In fact, it was smaller than just the living room of my apartment in New York. I lived alone in that apartment, but in my friends' apartment three of us had to live together.

We took our shoes off at the door, sat down on the floor, and talked for an hour. Then we spread mats for sleeping on the floor.

I was very tired from the long flight, but I couldn't fall asleep right away. I lay on my mat thinking about how different and how strange everything was.

The next morning when I woke up, I head the "ting, ting, ting" of a wind chime. I sat up and looked out the window. Rain was falling softly over a beautiful garden. I knew I was going to like living in Japan.

Find past tense verbs.

Fill in the blanks with the past tense of the verbs. You can find the answers in the preceding story.

Present Tense	Past Tense
get up	_____
sit down	_____
know	_____
lie	_____

Guess the meanings of words.

Read each section of the story. Circle the letter in front of the answers you think are correct. Try not to use a dictionary.

My plane arrived in the evening. I waited in my seat until the plane stopped. Then I got up and followed the other passengers off the plane.

Inside the terminal, I saw signs written in Japanese. I heard people speaking. . . .

1. The airplane *arrived* means
   a. the airplane went away from the airport.
   b. the airplane came to the airport.

2. A *terminal* is
   a. a building where passengers get on and off airplanes.
   b. a building where passengers park their cars.

I heard people speaking Japanese fluently. Even little children, only two or three years old, were speaking Japanese much better than I could. And I had been trying so hard to learn it!

3. People who speak a language *fluently*
   a. do not speak the language well.
   b. speak the language well.

4. When people *try hard* to learn a language,
   a. they study that language very much.
   b. they don't study that language very much.

Everything I looked at interested me. I saw streets that were narrow and crowded with people and cars. I saw buses and trains everywhere.

5. When a street is *crowded* with people and cars,
   a. there are few people and cars in the street.
   b. there are many people and cars in the street.

We took our shoes off at the door, sat down on the floor, and talked for an hour. Then we spread mats for sleeping on the floor.

6. When Mary and her friends *spread* the mats on the floor,
   a. they picked up the mats from the floor.
   b. they put the mats down on the floor.

I was very tired from the long flight, but I couldn't go to sleep right away. I lay on my mat thinking about how different and how strange everything was.

7. *Right away* means

   a. soon.
   b. not soon.

8. When Mary says everything was *strange*, she means:

   a. This was the first time that she had visited Japan, so everything was new and different to her.
   b. Mary had seen everything many times before, so she knew about everything.

The next morning when I woke up, I heard the "ting, ting, ting" of a wind chime. I sat up and looked out the window. Rain was falling softly over a beautiful garden. I knew I was going to like living in Japan.

9. "Ting, ting, ting" is

   a. the sound a wind chime makes.
   b. the sound of the rain.

Use words in context.

Fill in the blanks with one of the following words or expressions.

crowded   fluently   terminal   tried hard

The _____ was _____ with people who were speaking Japanese _____. Mary _____ _____ to understand what they were saying, but she couldn't understand one word.

strange   ting, ting, ting

Outside the window was a _____ world. She heard the _____ of a wind chime and saw rain falling on a garden.

Check your comprehension.

*Read each section of the story. Then put **T** in front of statements that are true. Put **F** in front of statements that are false.*

I remember my first hours in Japan.

My plane arrived in the evening. I waited in my seat until the plane stopped. Then I got up and followed the other passengers off the plane.

_____ 1. Mary got up from her seat before the plane stopped.

Inside the terminal, I saw signs written in Japanese. I heard people speaking Japanese fluently. Even little children, only two or three years old, were speaking Japanese much better than I could. And I had been trying so hard to learn it!

_____ 2. Mary spoke more Japanese than small children did.

_____ 3. Mary probably studied Japanese for a long time before coming to Japan.

From the car, I saw a new world. Everything I looked at interested me. I saw streets that were narrow and crowded with people and cars. I saw buses and trains everywhere.

_____ 4. Mary was riding in a car.

The apartment was very small. In fact, it was smaller than just the living room of my apartment in New York. I lived alone in that apartment, but in my friends' apartment three of us had to live together.

_____ 5. The living room of her apartment in New York was larger than her friends' apartment.

_____ 6. Three people lived in the apartment in Japan.

We took our shoes off at the door, sat down on the floor, and talked for an hour. Then we spread mats for sleeping on the floor.

_____ 7. They did not wear shoes in the apartment.

_____ 8. Mary slept on a mat.

I was very tired from the long flight, but I couldn't go to sleep right away. I lay on my mat thinking about how different and how strange everything was.

_____ 9. Mary was very tired, but she didn't go to sleep right away because she was thinking about many things.

The next morning when I woke up, I heard the "ting, ting, ting" of a wind chime. I sat up and looked out the window. Rain was falling softly over a beautiful garden. I knew I was going to like living in Japan.

_____ 10. Mary didn't like the wind chime, the rain, and the garden.

Determine the meanings of pronouns.

Circle the letter in front of the word that has the same meaning as the word just before the parenthesis. The first two are done for you as examples.

Inside the terminal, I saw signs written in Japanese. I heard people speaking Japanese fluently. Even little children, only two or three years old, were speaking Japanese much better than I could. And I had been trying so hard to learn it ((a.) Japanese   b. English)!

I was excited, but a little lonely and afraid. How happy I was when I heard two American friends who (a. Mary   (b.) Mary's friends) had come to meet me call out, "Mary! Mary! Long time no see!"

My friends took me to their (a. Mary's friends'   b. Mary's) apartment. From the car, I saw a new world. Everything I looked at interested me (a. Mary   b. Mary's friends). I saw streets that were narrow and crowded with people and cars. I saw buses and trains everywhere.

The apartment was very small. In fact, it (a. apartment in Japan   b. apartment in New York) was smaller than just the living room of my (a. Mary's   b. friends') apartment in New York. I lived alone in that apartment, but in my friends' apartment three of us (a. Mary   b. Mary and her friends) had to live together.

We (a. Mary   b. Mary and her friends) took our shoes off at the door, sat down on the floor, and talked for an hour. Then we (a. Mary   b. Mary and her friends) spread mats for sleeping on the floor.

I was very tired from the long flight, but I couldn't go to sleep right away. I lay on my mat thinking about how different and how strange everything was.

Use words in context.

Write one word or expression in each blank.

apartment	everywhere	met	narrow	took

Two American friends _____ Mary at the airport. They _____ her to their _____. From the car, Mary saw _____ streets filled with thousands of people. There were cars, buses, and trains _____.

sat down	small	took off

The apartment was very _____. Mary and her friends _____ their shoes, _____ on the floor, and talked for about an hour before they went to bed.

different   right away   strange   tired   woke up

Mary was _____, but she couldn't sleep
_____ because she was thinking about how
_____ and _____ everything was.

The next morning, it was raining when Mary _____.
She looked out the window and saw a beautiful garden, and she heard
a wind chime ringing.

Mary knew that she was going to like living in Japan.

Use information to make guesses.

Read the paragraphs. Then answer the question following each paragraph.

(1) Inside the terminal, I saw signs written in Japanese. (2) I heard people speaking Japanese fluently. (3) Even little children, only two or three years old, were speaking Japanese much better than I could. (4) And I had been trying so hard to learn it!

Which sentences tell you that Mary studied Japanese before she went to Japan? (   ) (   )

I was excited, but a little lonely and afraid. How happy I was when I heard two American friends who had come to meet me call out "Mary! Mary! Long time no see!"

Why was Mary happy when she heard her American friends? (Choose two answers.)

a. because she was feeling lonely and afraid
b. because she wanted to see her friends
c. because she was excited

(1) The next morning when I woke up, I heard the "ting, ting, ting" of a wind chime. (2) I sat up and looked out the window. (3) Rain was falling softly over a beautiful garden. (4) I knew I was going to like living in Japan.

Which sentence tells you that Mary liked the wind chime, the rain, and the garden? (   )

Discuss feelings.

1. How did Mary feel her first night and first morning in Japan?
2. Have you traveled alone? Where did you go? How did you get there? How did you feel when you got there?

Summarize the reading.

Fill in the blanks with the phrases listed. Do this exercise two times. Do it orally the first time; write it out the second time.

a beautiful garden	in the evening
a new world	like living
a wind chime	on mats
at the airport	speaking Japanese
for an hour	their apartment
how different	very small
how strange	when Mary woke up
in Japanese	

Mary arrived at the airport _____. In the terminal, she saw signs written _____, and people were _____. Two friends met Mary _____ _____. They took Mary to _____. From the car, Mary saw _____. The apartment was _____. Mary and her friends talked _____ _____. Then they went to sleep _____. Mary couldn't sleep right away. She thought about _____ _____ and _____ everything was. The next morning _____, she heard _____ _____. She looked out the window and saw rain falling on _____. She knew that she was going to _____ _____ in Japan.

Part Three — CULTURE SHOCK

Listening

Listen for the main idea.

Your teacher will give you some information. Listen to the information. Then answer the following question.

What is the information about? (Circle the letter in front of the correct answer.)

a. how you feel when you are at home in your country

b. how you feel when you go to a new country

Listen for words.

Fill in the blanks while listening to the information again. Use the following words and expressions.

bad feelings   for example
differences   good feelings
different   hate

When you go to a new country, you find many things that are
_____. People may speak a _____
language, _____, and their way of thinking and doing
things may be _____. These _____ give
you _____ and _____. You may like the
new language, _____, but you may _____
the way people look at you. *Culture shock* is when you get these kinds of
feelings.

Find opposite words.

Write one word in each blank. You will find the words you need in the preceding exercise.

Opposite Word

same   _____

good   _____

old   _____

Check your comprehension.

Your teacher will tell you the information again. Answer the following questions while listening. Circle the letter in front of the correct answer.

1. What is culture shock?

    a. a language that you learn in a new country
    b. feelings that you have when things are different
    c. a new way of thinking and doing things

2. When do you experience culture shock?

    a. when you are in a place where everything is the same
    b. when you are in a place where many things are different

3. What kinds of feelings do you have when you have culture shock?

    a. only good feelings
    b. good and bad feelings
    c. only bad feelings

Reading

Preview the reading.

Look at the reading. Find and circle the following words.

At first   Later   Finally

These words are important in the reading. Each of them introduces a new idea about culture shock.

Find key phrases.

Find and underline the following phrases.

Culture shock!
. . . happens when you live in another country
People . . . different language
think and act differently
first, differences . . . interesting . . . amusing
Later, you . . . dislike . . . differences
They . . . no longer amusing . . . interesting
Finally, after . . . long time,
get used to . . . people . . . way of life
You . . . accept . . . new life,
become part of it

Culture Shock

Culture shock! It happens when you go to live in another country. People speak a different language. They think and act differently.

At first, you think the differences are interesting or, perhaps, amusing. You laugh at the way people do things. You say, "That's not how we do it at home."

Later, however, you begin to dislike some of the differences. They are no longer amusing or interesting to you. You complain about them. You get homesick and wish you could go back home where people do things the "right" way.

Finally, after you are in the country a long time, you get used to the people and their way of life. You learn to accept the new life, and you begin to become part of it.

Check your comprehension.

Refer to the key phrases you underlined and answer the following questions.

1. What is the reading about?
   a. differences
   b. people
   c. culture shock
   d. other countries

2. How do you feel first about the differences?
   a. You feel they are interesting and amusing.
   b. You dislike them.
   c. You accept them.

3. How do you feel a little later?
   a. You feel they are interesting and amusing.
   b. You dislike them.
   c. You accept them.

4. How do you feel after a long time?
   a. You feel they are interesting and amusing.
   b. You dislike them.
   c. You accept them.

Find opposite words.

Write one word in each blank. The words you need are in the key phrases you underlined in the reading.

Opposite Word

not funny   _____

like   _____

uninteresting   _____

Make words negative.

Look at the words uninteresting *and* dislike. Un- *and* dis- *make the words negative. Now can you explain the meaning of these two words?*

uninteresting = _____

dislike   = _____

Define words.

Match the word or phrase on the left with one of the definitions on the right.

_____ complain

_____ get homesick

_____ get used to

a. learn to accept or to like something

b. say that something is bad

c. wish strongly to go home

Use information from the reading.

Fill in the chart with information from the reading.

CULTURE SHOCK

STAGE	TIME IN THE COUNTRY	FEELINGS
1	at first	a. interesting b.
2		a. b.
3		a.

Discuss living in a new place.

Have you ever lived in another city or country for a long time? How did you feel when you first arrived there? How did you feel later? Did you like living there? Why, or why not?

Part Four

Outside Reading

Find information about a country.

Is there a country you have traveled to? Or is there a country you would like to travel to? Look up that country in an encyclopedia. Find the following information about that country and share the information with your classmates.

Name of country   _____

Population (number of people)   _____

Area (number of square miles)   _____

Name of the largest city   _____

Main industry   _____

Share your information with your classmates.

Lesson 3

Part One — WORLD CLIMATES

Listening

Listen for the main idea.

Your teacher will give you some information. Listen to the information. Then answer the following question.

What is the information about? (Circle the letter in front of the correct answer.)

a. the north and south poles

b. two different climates

Listen for words.

Fill in the blanks while listening to the information again. Use the following words and expressions.

cold	north and south
equator	polar
hot	tropical

Some parts of the word are _____ all year. These places have a _____ climate and are near the _____ _____. Other parts of the world are _____ all year. These places have a _____ climate and are near the _____ poles.

Use words in context.

Write one of the following words or expressions in each blank.

equator   south pole   tropical
north pole   polar (2)

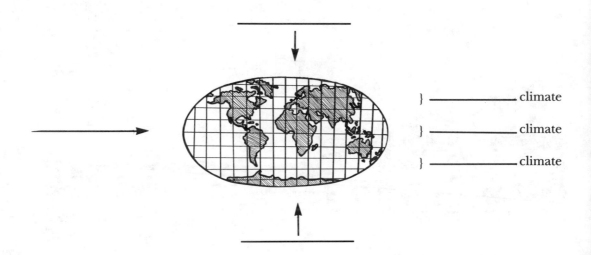

Check your comprehension.

Your teacher will ask you some questions about the information. Listen to the questions. Then fill in the blanks using the following words.

cold   equator   hot   north and south poles

1. Tropical climates are near the _____.
2. They have _____ weather all year.
3. Polar climates are near the _____.
4. They have _____ weather all year.

Listen to the information again. Check your answers while you listen.

Reading

Preview the reading.

Look at the chart. Then answer the following questions.

1. What does the chart show?
   a. climate
   b. distance
   c. years

2. List the five major types of climates.
   a. _____tropical humid_____
   b. _____
   c. _____
   d. _____
   e. _____

3. Look at the tropical humid climates. List the four kinds of tropical humid climates.
   a. _____tropical wet_____
   b. _____
   c. _____
   d. _____

4. Look at the tropical wet and dry climate. What city is listed as an example weather station? What country is that city in?

WORLD CLIMATES

CLIMATE	WEATHER STATION	AVERAGE ANNUAL TEMPERATURE (Fahrenheit degrees)	AVERAGE ANNUAL PRECIPITATION (inches)
Tropical Humid Climates			
Tropical wet	Singapore	80.1	92.9
Tropical wet and dry	Cuiaba, Brazil	80	54.6
Low-latitude desert	William Creek, Australia	68	5.4
Low-latitude steppe	Benghazi, Libya	69	11.9

WORLD CLIMATES

CLIMATE	WEATHER STATION	AVERAGE ANNUAL TEMPERATURE (Fahrenheit degrees)	AVERAGE ANNUAL PRECIPITATION (inches)
Dry Climates			
Middle-latitude desert	Fallon, Nevada, U.S.A.	50.6	4.7
Middle-latitude steppe	Williston, North Dakota, U.S.A.	39.2	14.4
Humid Mesothermal Climates			
Dry-summer subtropical	Perth, Australia	64	33.9
Humid subtropical	Shanghai, China	49	45.8
Marine	Paris, France	50.5	22.6
Humid Microthermal Climates			
Humid continental			
Warm summer	Bucharest, Rumania	51	23.0
Cool summer	Montreal, Canada	42	41.0
Subarctic	Moose Factory, Canada	30	21.0
Polar Climates			
Tundra	Upernivik, Greenland	16	9.2
Ice-cap	Little America, Antarctica	− 11.3	No data

Adapted from *Physical Elements of Geography* by Vernon C. Finch, Glenn T. Trewartha, Arthur H. Robinson and Edwin H. Hammond. Copyright 1957, McGraw-Hill Books Co., Inc. Reproduced by permission of McGraw-Hill Publishing Company.

Guess the meanings of words.

Read the information. Then circle the letter in front of the correct answer. For some questions, more than one answer may be correct.

Rain and snow are two forms of precipitation. Rain occurs when the temperature is above freezing (32°F or 0°C). Snow occurs when the temperature is below freezing.

   1. Which of the following show temperature?
     a. 35°F
     b. 35 km
     c. 35°C
     d. 1988

   2. Which of the following is precipitation?
     a. heat
     b. snow
     c. rain
     d. steam

Look at these numbers: 2, 4, 6, 8, 10. The average number is 6. (2 + 4 + 6 + 8 + 10 = 30, and 30 ÷ 5 = 6).

   3. Look at these numbers: 1, 2, 3, 6. What is the average of these numbers?
     a. 3
     b. 6
     c. 12

Annual means "for one year."

   4. *Average annual temperature* means
     a. the average temperature for one month.
     b. the average temperature for one year.

Use words in context.

Write one of the following words or expressions in each blank.

         average (2)   annual   precipitation

The _____ _____ temperature in
Shanghai is 49 degrees. The _____ annual
_____ is 45.8 inches.

Find specific information.

Answer the following questions. You will find the information you need in the world climate chart.

1. The average annual temperature in Singapore is 80.1°F. What is the average annual temperature in Benghazi, Libya?

2. The average annual precipitation in Singapore is 92.9 inches. What is the average annual precipitation in Cuiaba, Brazil?

3. Which station has the warmest average annual temperature? Which has the coldest?

4. Which has the highest average annual precipitation? Which has the lowest?

5. Which station gets more rain, Shanghai or Paris?

Use words in context.

Write one word in each blank.

climate   example   listed

Benghazi, Libya, is _____ as an _____
station of a low-latitude steppe _____.

Use information to make guesses.

*Put **T** in front of the statement you think is true. Put **F** in front of the statement you think is false. Refer to the chart for information.*

_____ 1. People living in Fallon, Nevada, should probably carry an umbrella with them every day.

_____ 2. Tropical wet climates get less rain than humid subtropical climates.

Discuss climates.

1. Do you live in a hot climate or a cold climate? Tell about the different seasons (spring, summer, winter, fall). Are they hot or cold? Is there a lot of rain? When? Does it snow? When?

2. If you think only about climate, which of the places on the chart would you like to live in? Why?

Part Two — THE FRIENDS ON THE FROZEN LAKE

Listening

Listen for the main idea.

Your teacher will tell you a story. Listen to the story. Then answer the following question.

What is the story about? (Circle the letter in front of the correct answer.)

a. growing up in Wisconsin

b. walking on ice

Listen for words.

Fill in the blanks while listening to the story again. Use the following words and expressions.

afraid	grew up	warm
cold	ice	water
fall	kidding	

Sam _____ in Florida where the winters are

_____. One day, he moved to Wisconsin where the winters

are very _____.

He lived in an apartment with John. One winter day John said,

"Let's go on a hike. I'll show you how to walk on _____."

Sam thought John was _____, but he went on the

hike with him.

They came to a lake. It was covered with _____.

John began to walk across the lake. He told Sam to come, but Sam

didn't want to. He was _____ that he would

_____ into the lake.

Guess the meanings of words.

Read the information. Then answer the questions.

Sam grew up in Florida. He was born in Florida and lived there until he was 21 years old.

1. Sam *grew up* in Florida means that
   a. Sam lived in Florida all the time that he was a child.
   b. Sam was born in Florida, but he lived somewhere else when he was a child.

John said, "I'll show you how to walk on water." Sam said, "You must be kidding."

2. Sam thought that John was *kidding*. He thought that John
   a. was telling a joke and wasn't going to walk on water.
   b. really was going to walk on water.

The lake was covered with ice. John began to walk across the lake, but Sam was afraid that he would fall in.

3. *Covered with ice* means that
   a. some parts had ice; some parts had no ice.
   b. there was ice everywhere—all over the lake.

Use words in context.

Write one word or phrase in each blank.

ice   just kidding   water

John said, "I'll show you how to walk on _____."
But he was _____. He wasn't going to do that! He was
going to show Sam how to walk on _____.

afraid   fall   grew up   ice

Sam _____ in Florida, so walking across
_____ was a new experience for him. That is why he was
_____. He thought he might _____ into
the lake.

Check your comprehension.

*Your teacher will ask you some questions about the story. Listen to the
questions. Then fill in the blanks using the following words.*

afraid   Florida   lake   Wisconsin
cold   hike   warm

1. He grew up in _____.
2. They are very _____.
3. He moved to _____.
4. They are very _____.
5. They went on a _____.
6. He walked across a frozen _____.
7. He was _____.

Listen to the information again. Check your answers while you listen.

Reading

Preview the reading.

Read the story quickly. Then answer the following questions.

1. Did Sam walk across the lake?

2. How did Sam feel later? Why did he feel that way?

3. What did John tell Sam then?

The Friends on the Frozen Lake

Sam grew up in Florida. He lived there until he was 21 years old. Then he moved to Wisconsin to take a new job.

Sam's first winter in Wisconsin was a new experience for him. He had never lived anywhere before where it became so cold.

One Saturday in the middle of January, Sam's roommate John asked, "How about going on a hike today?"

"Go on a hike today? A hike on a cold day like today?" Sam replied.

"Sure," John answered. "Come hiking with me, and I'll show you how to walk on water."

"Walk on water? You must be kidding."

John and Sam put on thick coats, gloves, hats, and high boots. They got into John's car, drove about 10 miles into the country, and parked the car beside the road. Then they hiked through the forest in snow that came up to their knees.

After a while, they came to a large, frozen lake. "Now, let's walk on water," John said.

"Walk on the lake?" Sam asked. "Are you sure the ice is strong enough to hold us?"

"Come on! You're afraid," John told him.

"The ice might break. I might fall in," said Sam.

But John didn't hear him. He was already far out on the ice, walking toward the middle of the lake.

Sam didn't want to be left alone. He stepped carefully onto the ice. It was hard; he didn't fall in.

"Don't go out to the middle," Sam shouted to John. "I want to be close to shore if the ice breaks." But John was already on the other side of the lake.

Slowly, Sam walked across the lake. The ice didn't break, and Sam didn't fall in.

Later, Sam felt foolish for being afraid. But John told him, "Look, it's OK to be afraid sometimes—especially when you are experiencing something new."

Guess the meanings of words.

Read each section of the story. Then circle the letter in front of the correct answer.

Sam grew up in Florida. He lived there until he was 21 years old. Then he moved to Wisconsin to take a new job.

1. *Then he moved to Wisconsin* means that
    a. Sam was visiting Wisconsin. He was going to stay only a short time.
    b. Sam was going to live in Wisconsin for a long time.

Sam's first winter in Wisconsin was a new experience for him. He had never lived anywhere before where it became so cold.

2. The winter in Wisconsin was a *new experience* for Sam means that
    a. Sam had been in Wisconsin during the winter before.
    b. this was Sam's first time in Wisconsin during the winter

One Saturday in the middle of January, Sam's roommate John asked, "How about going on a hike today?"

3. *Middle of January* means
    a. about January 1.
    b. about January 15.
    c. about January 30.

They got into John's car, drove about 10 miles into the country. . . . Then they hiked through the forest. . . .
After a while, they came to a large, frozen lake.

4. *After a while* means
    a. later, after some time passed.
    b. right away, very soon.

"Don't go out to the middle," Sam shouted to John. "I want to be close to shore if the ice breaks." But John was already on the other side of the lake.

5. The *shore* of the lake is
    a. the land around the lake.
    b. the water near the middle of the lake.

Later, Sam felt foolish for being afraid. But John told him, "Look, it's OK to be afraid sometimes—especially when you are experiencing something new."

6. *Later* means the time

  a. while they were crossing the lake.
  b. after they crossed the lake.

7. When Sam felt *foolish*, he felt

  a. good
  b. bad

Use words in context.

Write one word or expression in each blank.

afraid   moved
foolish   new experience
later   shore
middle of

Sam _____ to Wisconsin from Florida. Therefore, walking across a lake in the _____ the winter was a _____ for him. At first, Sam was afraid, but after a while, he walked to the _____ on the other side of the lake. _____, he felt _____ for being _____.

Check your comprehension.

*Read each section of the story. Then read the statements following each section. Put **T** in front of each statement you think is true. Put **F** in front of each statement you think is false.*

One Saturday in the middle of January, Sam's roommate John said, "How about going on a hike today?"

_____ 1. John said, "Let's go on a hike today."
_____ 2. John asked, "What do you want to do today?"

"Go on a hike today? A hike on a cold day like today?" Sam asked.

_____ 3. Sam thinks it is too cold to go hiking.
_____ 4. Sam thinks it is a good day to go hiking.

"Sure," John answered.

_____ 5. John said "Yes."
_____ 6. John said "No."

"Come hiking with me, and I'll show you how to walk on water."

_____ 7. John really means that they will walk on water.
_____ 8. John really means that they will walk across a frozen lake.

John and Sam put on heavy coats, gloves, hats, and high boots. They got into John's car, drove about 10 miles into the country, and parked the car beside the road. Then they hiked through the forest in snow that came up to their knees.

_____ 9. There was only a little snow.
_____ 10. There was a lot of snow. The snow was deep.

"Walk on the lake?" Sam asked. "Are you sure the ice is strong enough to hold us?"
"Come on! You're afraid," John told him.

_____ 11. John is saying, "Let's go back to the car because you are afraid."
_____ 12. John is saying, "Stop being afraid and come on the ice with me."

"The ice might break. I might fall in," said Sam.
But John didn't hear him. He was already far out on the ice, walking toward the middle of the lake.
Sam didn't want to be left behind. He stepped carefully onto the ice. It was hard; he didn't fall in.

_____ 13. Sam didn't want to be alone on the shore.
_____ 14. Sam wanted to be by himself.

Determine the meanings of pronouns.

Circle the letter in front of the word that has the same meaning as the word just before the parentheses.

One Saturday in the middle of January, Sam's roommate John asked, "How about going on a hike today?"
"Go on a hike today? A hike on a cold day like today?" Sam replied.

"Sure," John answered. "Come hiking with me (a. Sam   b. John), and I'll (a. Sam   b. John) show you (a. Sam   b. John) how to walk on water."

"Walk on water? You (a. Sam   b. John) must be joking."

John and Sam put on thick coats, gloves, hats, and high boots. They (a. coats, hats, and gloves   b. Sam and John) got into John's car, drove about 10 miles into the country. . . .

. . . "Now, let's walk on water," John said.

"Walk on the lake?" Sam asked. "Are you (a. Sam   b. John) sure the ice is strong enough to hold us?"

"Come on! You're (a. Sam   b. John) afraid," John told him.

"The ice might break. I (a. Sam   b. John) might fall in," said Sam.

But John didn't hear him (a. Sam   b. John). He (a. Sam   b. John) was already far out on the ice, walking toward the middle of the lake.

Sam didn't want to be left alone. He (a. Sam   b. John) stepped carefully onto the ice. It (a. Sam   b. ice) was hard; he (a. Sam   b. John) didn't fall in.

"Don't go out to the middle," Sam shouted to John. "I (a. Sam   b. John) want to be close to shore if the ice breaks." But John was already on the other side of the lake.

Slowly, Sam walked across the lake. The ice didn't break, and he (a. Sam   b. John) didn't fall in.

Summarize the reading.

Complete the following sentences. Do this exercise two times. Do it orally the first time; do it in writing the second time.

1. Sam grew up _____.
2. When he was 21, he _____.
3. The first Wisconsin winter was _____.
4. One day, Sam and his roommate John went _____.
5. They walked across _____.
6. Sam was afraid, but he didn't want to be left _____.
7. Later, Sam felt _____.
8. But John told him _____.

Discuss an experience.

1. Do you think it is all right to be afraid sometimes? Why, or why not? Do you think it was OK for Sam to be afraid?

2. Tell about a new experience you had. What happened? How did you feel?

Part Three — LONGITUDE AND LATITUDE

Listening

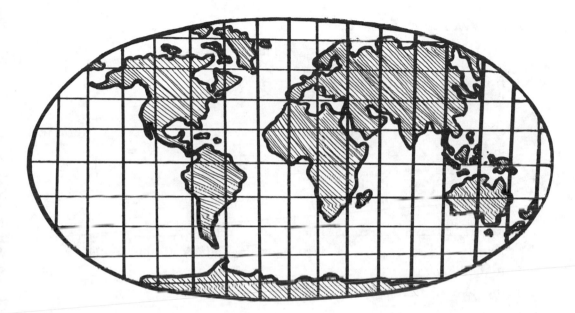

Listen for the main idea.

Your teacher will give you some information. Listen to the information. Then answer the following question.

What is the information about? (Circle the letter in front of the correct answer.)

a. world climate

b. a man who walked on ice for the first time

c. the lines on a map

Listen for words.

Listen to the information again. Write one of the following words or phrases in each blank while listening.

climate	locate
horizontal lines	longitude
latitude	time

A map has vertical lines and horizontal lines. The vertical lines show

_____. The _____ show _____

_____. Using these lines, we can _____ any place on

earth. We can also determine what _____ it is at that place, and we can guess about the _____ there.

Listen to the information again. Check your answers while listening.

Use words in context.

Write one word or expression in each blank.

from one side to the other side
from top to bottom

Vertical lines on a map run _____. Horizontal lines run _____.

earth	location	place
horizontal	map	vertical

The _____ lines on a _____ show latitude.
The _____ lines show longitude. You can use these lines to determine the _____ of any _____ on the _____.

Check your comprehension.

Your teacher will ask you some questions about the information. Listen to the questions. Then fill in the blanks using the following words.

climate	location	vertical
horizontal	time	

1. The _____ lines show latitude.
2. The _____ lines show longitude.
3. These lines help us determine _____, _____, and _____.

Listen to the information again. Check your answers while you listen.

Reading

Find key phrases.

Read the information quickly. Do not read every word. Then find the answers to the following questions.

1. What do latitude and longitude together help us determine?

2. What does longitude help us determine?

3. What does latitude help us determine?

Longitude and Latitude

Look at a map of the earth or a globe. You will notice that there are vertical and horizontal lines. The vertical lines show longitude. The horizontal lines show latitude.

Location

Longitude shows the number of degrees a place is east or west of Greenwich, England. Latitude shows the number of degrees a place is north or south of the equator. Low latitudes are close to the equator. High latitudes are near the polar regions.

You can locate any place on earth if you know the longitude and latitude. Mexico City, for example, is about 98 degrees west of Greenwich and about 19 degrees north of the equator. Cairo is near 32 degrees longitude and 30 degrees latitude.

Time

Time is measured from zero degrees longitude, which runs through Greenwich, England. For every 15 degrees you travel east or west of Greenwich, time changes by one hour. It increases if you travel east. It decreases if you travel west. For example, New York City is approximately 77 degrees west of Greenwich. Seventy-seven divided by 15 is 5.1. Therefore, when it is 12 noon in Greenwich, it is 7 A.M. in New York.

Climate

In general, you can determine the climate of an area if you know the latitude. For example, tropical areas are in low latitudes. They tend to have warm to hot temperatures all year. The polar regions of the Arctic and Antarctic are in high latitudes. These areas have cold temperatures all year. The middle latitudes, which are the areas between the tropics and the polar regions, generally have warm to hot summers and cold winters.

Guess the meanings of words.

*Read the information. Then read the statements following the information. Put **T** in front of each statement that is true. Put **F** in front of each statement that is false.*

Look at the two sets of numbers. The first set of numbers increases from 1 to 5; the second set decreases from 5 to 1.

1, 2, 3, 4, 5   5, 4, 3, 2, 1

_____ 1. *Increase* means "to become smaller."

_____ 2. *Decrease* means "to become larger."

_____ 3. *Increase* means "to become larger"; *decrease* means "to become smaller."

We use degrees to measure temperature. We also use degrees to show location on a map.

_____ 4. We learn how hot or cold something is when we measure its temperature.

_____ 5. We can use degrees to find a city, for example, on a map.

_____ 6. 78°F means 78 degrees Fahrenheit.

_____ 7. When we say that a place is 70 degrees west of Greenwich, we mean that the temperature there is 70 degrees Fahrenheit.

Use words in context.

Write one word in each blank.

decreases   degrees   increases   measure

1. A circle has 360 _____.

2. We can _____ distance.

3. Here are two sets of numbers: 0,1,2,3,4,5 and 5,4,3,2,1,0. The first set _____ from 0 to 5. The second set _____ _____ from 5 to 0.

Find key words and phrases.

Look back at the reading. Find and underline the answers to the following questions. Do not write out the answers.

1. What does longitude show?

2. What does latitude show?

3. Where is time measured from?

4. If you travel 15 degrees east, do you gain time or lose time? How much time do you gain or lose?

5. If you travel 15 degrees west, how much time do you gain or lose?

6. Which can help you determine climate, longitude or latitude?

7. Where are tropical areas?

8. What is the climate like in tropical areas?

9. Where are polar regions?

10. What is the climate like in polar regions?

11. What is the climate like in middle latitudes?

Use the reading to solve problems.

Write out answers to the following questions.

1. What is the longitude of Greenwich, England?

2. What is the latitude of the equator?

3. The time difference between San Francisco and New York City is three hours. About how many degrees longitude is San Francisco from New York? (You don't have to look at a map to answer this question.)

4. If a place is at 45 degrees latitude, will its winters be hot or cold? How about its summers?

Summarize the reading.

Use the following questions to guide you in summarizing the reading. Do this exercise two times. Do it orally the first time; do it in writing the second time. Do not write the questions, only the answers.

1. What kinds of lines are there on a map or a globe?

2. What are the lines called?

3. What three things do the lines help you determine?

Discuss the location and climate of your hometown.

At about what latitude and longitude is your hometown? What kind of climate do you have there? How are the summers? How are the winters? What is the time difference between your town and Greenwich, England?

Part Four

Outside Reading

Find more information about a city on the chart.

Look up in an encyclopedia one of the cities listed in the chart on page 44. Try to find additional information about temperatures and precipitation there. Also, if there is a picture of the city, make a photocopy to bring to class to share with your classmates.

Lesson 4

Part One — WATERFOWL

Listening

Listen for the main idea.

Your teacher will give you some information. Listen to the information. Then answer the following question.

What is the information about? (Circle the letter in front of the correct answer.)

a. water

b. birds

Listen for words.

Fill in the blanks while listening to the information again. Use the following words and expressions.

a number of ways	including
differ	near
feeding habits	waterfowl

Waterfowl are birds that live in or _____ water. Swans, geese, and ducks are three kinds of _____. They _____ from each other in _____, _____ size, color, and _____. Some _____ are very large birds.

Guess the meanings of words.

*Read the information. Then read the statements following the information. Put **T** in front of statements that are true. Put **F** in front of statements that are false.*

Some birds are called waterfowl. These birds like to live around water. They fly above the water. They swim in it. Some of these birds dive into the water to get food.

_____   1.   Birds that live around water are called waterfowl.

_____   2.   Some waterfowl go into the water to get food.

_____   3.   *Dive into the water* means "go into the water."

_____   4.   Waterfowl cannot swim.

The feeding habits of waterfowl differ. Some waterfowl dive for food. Some of them just put their head and neck underwater. Some of them eat grass and seeds on land.

_____   5.   *Feeding habits* refers to the way waterfowl drink water.

_____   6.   *Feeding habits* refers to the way waterfowl eat.

_____   7.   Things that *differ* are not the same.

Waterfowl differ in a number of ways, including size, color, and feeding habits.

_____   8.   *A number of ways* means "one way."

_____   9.   When we say that things differ in *a number of ways*, we mean that they differ in many ways.

_____ 10. Size, color, and feeding habits are three ways in which water-fowl differ.

_____ 11. The word *include* groups things together.

_____ 12. Waterfowl are of different sizes, different colors, and have different feeding habits.

Waterfowl are usually near water. You can often see them swimming or feeding in the water.

_____ 13. Waterfowl are usually far from water.

Use words in context.

Write one word or expression in each blank.

a number of ways	dive
differ	feeding habits

The _____ _____ of waterfowl _____ _____ in _____ . Some birds _____ _____ for food; others eat on land.

include	near	waterfowl

_____ _____ _____ _____ swans, ducks, and geese.
These birds live _____ water.

Check your comprehension.

Your teacher will ask you some questions about the information. Listen to the questions. Then fill in the blanks using the following words.

color	feeding habits	size	water
ducks	geese	swans	

1. They live in or near _____ .
2. They are _____ , _____ , and _____ .
3. They differ in _____ , _____ , and _____ .

Listen to the information again. Check your answers while you listen.

Reading

Preview the reading.

Read through the following chart quickly. Do not try to understand every word. Look for the answers to the following questions.

1. How many different kinds of waterfowl are listed in the chart?
2. How many kinds of ducks are listed in the chart?

WATERFOWL

SWANS

Body:	Very large, larger than geese. Have longer necks than geese.
Sexes:	Males and females look alike.
Food:	Eat water plants and seeds.
Feeding:	Put their head and neck underwater to feed.
Flight:	Fly in V formations or in lines.
Other:	Adults are all white.

GEESE

Body:	Larger and heavier than ducks; have a longer neck than ducks.
Sexes:	Males and females look alike.
Food:	Eat grass, seeds, and water plants.
Feeding:	Feed mostly on land.
Flight:	Fly in V formations.

DUCKS

Marsh Ducks

Body:	Smaller than swans or geese.
Sexes:	Males and females do not look alike.
Food:	Eat water plants, seeds, grass, small water animals, and insects.
Feeding:	Feed on the surface of creeks, marshes, and ponds by putting bill into the water slightly and then raising it up into the air.
Flight:	Take flight directly into the air.

Diving Ducks

Body:	Smaller than swans or geese.
Sexes:	Males and females do not look alike.
Food:	Eat small water animals and plants.
Feeding:	Feed by diving into the water.
Flight:	Take flight by hitting their feet repeatedly on the surface of the water.
Other:	Usually found by oceans.

Stiff-tailed Ducks

Body:	Heavy body with short wings.
Sexes:	Males and females do not look alike.
Food:	Eat water animals, water plants, and insects.
Feeding:	Dive underwater for food.
Flight:	Have trouble taking flight because of heavy body and short wings.

Mergansers

Body:	Long and slender.
Sexes:	Males and females do not look alike.
Food:	Feed on small fish.
Feeding:	Grab and hold fish with their bills.
Flight:	Take flight directly into the air; fly in small flocks or pairs.

Match expressions.

Write one word or expression in each blank.

alike   feed   take flight   trouble   water

Same Meaning

They look different.   They do not look

_____.

plants that grow in water   _____ plants

to eat   to _____

to go into the air   to _____

to have difficulty   to have _____

Find specific information.

Look at the chart. Then answer the following questions.

1. Which are the largest—swans, geese, or ducks?

2. Which are the smallest—swans, geese, or ducks?

3. Where do each of the following feed? What do they eat?

Bird	Feeding Place	Food
Swans	Water	Water plants, seeds
Geese	_____	_____
Marsh ducks	_____	_____
Diving ducks	_____	_____
Stiff-tailed ducks	_____	_____
Mergansers	_____	_____

4. Which waterfowl fly in rows or V formations?

5. Do the males and females of the following waterfowl look alike? Answer by circling yes or no.

Bird	Alike?	
Swans	yes	no
Geese	yes	no
Marsh ducks	yes	no
Diving ducks	yes	no
Stiff-tailed ducks	yes	no
Mergansers	yes	no

6. Which bird is all white?

7. Which duck dives for fish?

8. The chart mentions four different places where there is water. List those places on the lines below. (Hint: Look under "Marsh Ducks" and "Diving Ducks.")

   a. _____   c. _____
   b. _____   d. _____

Summarize the chart.

Fill in the blanks.

The chart shows _____ kinds of waterfowl.

They are _____, _____, and

_____. _____ kinds of ducks are listed.

They are _____, _____,

_____, and _____.

Recall the information.

Do not look back at the chart or at your summary. Try to tell in one or two sentences what the chart is about.

The chart lists three . . . .

Use the information to make guesses.

If you saw two swans standing next to each other, do you think it would be difficult to tell the male from the female? Why, or why not?

Part Two — THE STRANGER
IN THE FOREST

Listening

Listen for the main idea.

Your teacher will give you some information. Listen to the information.
Then answer the following question.

What is the information about? (Circle the letter in front of the correct answer.)

a. a cold, windy day in the forest

b. a woman who went hiking in the forest

Listen for words.

Fill in the blanks while listening to the information again. Use the following words and expressions.

behind her   lake
day off   newspaper reporter
ducks   pleasantly surprised
hiked   trail

A _____ had a _____ from work. She drove into the forest and _____ along a _____. She came to a _____ where some _____ were swimming. The reporter stood there for a long time watching the ducks. Suddenly, she heard something move _____. When she turned to see what was there, she was _____.

Guess the meanings of words.

*Read the information. Then read the statements following the information. Put **T** in front of each statement that is true. Put **F** in front of each statement that is false.*

The woman worked for the newspaper. Her job was to write news stories.

_____ 1. A newspaper reporter does not have a job.
_____ 2. A newspaper reporter works for a newspaper.
_____ 3. A newspaper reporter writes news stories.
_____ 4. When we say that we *work for* a newspaper, we mean that we have a job at that newspaper.

The reporter did not have to go to work that day. She had the day off. She drove into the forest, got out of her car, and hiked along a trail until she came to a lake.

_____ 5. You have to go to work when you have a *day off.*
_____ 6. *Hike* has about the same meaning as *walk.*
_____ 7. A *trail* is a wide road for cars.
_____ 8. A *trail* is a place for walking.

The reporter heard something behind her. When she turned to see what it was, she was pleasantly surprised.

_____ 9.   When something is *behind you*, you can see it without turning.

_____ 10.   You feel good when you are *pleasantly surprised*.

Use words in context.

Write one of the following words or expressions in each blank.

behind her	hiked	pleasantly surprised
day off from work	newspaper reporter	trail

On her _____, a _____ went into the forest. There she _____ along a _____ until she came to a lake. While she was watching some ducks, something moved _____. She was _____ when she turned to see what was there.

Check your comprehension.

Your teacher will ask you some questions about the information. Listen to the questions. Then fill in the blanks using the following words or expressions.

a lake	behind her	the forest
a long time	some ducks	

1. She went into _____.
2. She came to _____.
3. She saw _____.
4. She stayed for _____.
5. She heard something move _____.

Listen to the information again. Check your answers while you listen.

Reading

Preview the reading.

Read the story quickly. Then answer the following questions.

1. Where did the reporter go on her day off?

2. What did she come to?

3. What did she see there?

4. What stood there looking at her?

The Stranger in the Forest

It was a Saturday, and Sonya had the day off. She drove her car out of the small town in central Wisconsin where she worked as a newspaper reporter.

She drove deep into the forest that surrounded the town, away from the problems of her job.

About 10 miles out of town, she turned off the highway and followed a dirt road for several more miles. Then she parked her car alongside the road and got out.

She stood beside the car for a moment and listened. She heard the chirping of birds, the tinkling of water in a nearby stream, and the whistling of the wind as it passed above the trees. She heard no people, no cars, no trucks.

She started walking and followed a deer trail for about 30 minutes. It ended at a small lake. She stood there for a long time and watched a flock of ducks.

Suddenly, she heard something move behind her. She wondered what was there. She turned slowly in order not to frighten anything away. To her delight, she saw eight deer.

They were standing in a semicircle and looking at her—the stranger in the forest.

Guess the meanings of words.

Read each section of the story. Then circle the letter in front of the correct answers.

It was a Saturday, and Sonya had the day off. She drove her car out of the small town in central Wisconsin where she worked as a newspaper reporter.

1. *Central* means

  a. northern part.
  b. middle part.

She drove deep into the forest that surrounded the town, away from the problems of her job.

About 10 miles out of town, she turned off the highway and followed a dirt road for several more miles.

2. *She drove deep into the forest* means that

  a. she drove only a short distance into the forest.
  b. she drove far into the forest.

She stood there for a long time and watched a flock of ducks.

3. A *flock* of ducks is
   a. only one duck
   b. many ducks

To her delight, she saw eight deer.
They were standing in a semicircle and looking at her—the stranger in the forest.

4. The word *delight* tells us that she felt
   a. bad.
   b. good.

5. *Semi* means "half." A *semicircle* is
   a. a half circle.
   b. a complete circle.

Check your comprehension.

Read each section of the story. Then read the statements. Put T in front of each statement that is true. Put F in front of each statement that is false.

It was a Saturday, and Sonya had the day off. She drove her car out of the small town in central Wisconsin where she worked as a newspaper reporter.

_____ 1. The reporter was working that Saturday.

She drove deep into the forest that surrounded the town, away from the problems of her job.

_____ 2. She went far into the forest.
_____ 3. The town is in the middle of the forest.
_____ 4. Sonya thought about her work when she was in the forest.

About 10 miles out of town, she turned off the highway and followed a dirt road for several more miles. Then she parked her car alongside the road and got out.

_____ 5. She drove on two roads.

She stood beside the car for a moment and listened. She heard the chirping of birds, the tinkling of water in a nearby stream, and the whistling of the wind as it passed above the trees. She heard no people, no cars, no trucks.

_____ 6. Chirping, tinkling, and whistling are the sounds which birds, water, and wind make.

She started walking and followed a deer trail for about 30 minutes. It ended at a small lake. She stood there for a long time and watched a flock of ducks.

_____ 7. She walked where people usually walk.

_____ 8. There were many ducks.

Suddenly, she heard something move behind her. She wondered what was there. She turned slowly in order not to frighten anything away. To her delight, she saw eight deer.

_____ 9. If she turned quickly, the deer might run away.

They were standing in a semicircle and looking at her—the stranger in the forest.

_____ 10. The deer were standing all around Sonya.

Use information to make guesses.

Read the information. Then put **T** in front of the statements you think are true. Put **F** in front of the statements you think are false.

She started walking and followed a deer trail for about 30 minutes. It ended at a small lake. She stood there for a long time and watched a flock of ducks.

_____ 1. Deer probably followed the trail to get to the lake.

_____ 2. The ducks were probably swimming in the lake.

_____ 3. Sonya probably didn't like ducks.

They were standing in a semicircle and looking at her—the stranger in the forest.

_____ 4. A stranger is someone we know well.

_____ 5. In the story, Sonya is the stranger.

Use words in context.

Write one of the following words in each blank.

day off	ducks	something
deep	lake	stranger
deer	problems	trail
delight	reporter	

A newspaper _____ had the _____
and went _____ into the forest. She liked the forest
because it was a place where she could get away from the
_____ of her job.

She hiked along a deer _____ until she came to a
_____. She stood by the lake for a long time watching
some _____.

Suddenly, she heard _____ move behind her. She
turned slowly to see what was there. To her _____, she saw
eight _____. They were looking at her—the _____
in the forest.

Determine the meanings of pronouns.

*Write a word or phrase in each blank. The word or phrase should refer to
the word just before the parentheses. The first one is done for you as an
example.*

About 10 miles out of town, she turned off the highway and onto a dirt
road. She drove several miles further into the forest. Then she parked alongside
the road and got out of the car.

She stood there (*by the car*) for a moment and listened. She heard the
chirping of birds, the tinkling of water in a nearby stream, and the whistling of
the wind as it (_____) passed above the trees. She heard no people, no
cars, no trucks.

She followed a deer trail for about 30 minutes. It (_____)
ended at a small lake. She stood there (_____) for a long time and
watched a flock of ducks.

Suddenly, she heard something (_____) move behind her. She
wondered what was there. She turned slowly in order not to frighten anything
away. To her delight, she saw eight deer.

Summarize the story.

Complete the following sentences. Do this exercise two times. Do it orally the first time; do it in writing the second time.

(1) A newspaper reporter. . . . (2) She went deep. . . .
(3) She hiked along. . . . (4) She came to a. . . . (5) She watched some. . . .
(6) Suddenly, she heard. . . . (7) She turned. . . . (8) She saw. . . .
(9) They were. . . .

Discuss the story.

Why does the story say Sonya was the "stranger in the forest"? Tell (or write) about a time you were a stranger somewhere.

Part Three — **CANADA GOOSE**

Listening

Listen for the Main Idea.

Your teacher will give you some information. Listen to the information. Then answer the following question.

What is the information about? (Circle the letter in front of the correct answer.)

a. a bird that lives in the same place all year

b. a bird that lives in one place during the summer and another place during the winter

Listen for words.

Fill in the blanks while listening to the information again. Use the following words and expressions.

geese	north
goose	south
loud noise	travels
migratory	

The Canada _____ is a large bird of North America. It is a _____ bird which _____ _____ in the spring and _____ in the fall. It _____ together with many other Canada _____. It makes a _____ while it is flying. People on the ground can hear the noise.

Guess the meanings of words.

*Read the information. Then read the statements following the information. Put **T** in front of statements that are true. Put **F** in front of statements that are false.*

The Canada goose makes a loud noise when it flies. People on the ground can hear it.

_____ 1. *Noise* probably means the sound the goose makes with its mouth while it is flying.

_____ 2. People on the ground can hear the noise because it is loud.

_____ 3. It is difficult for people to hear a loud noise.

A migratory bird travels from one place to another place. The Canada goose, for example, is in the north during the summer and in the south during the winter.

_____ 4. A migratory bird stays in the same place all year.

_____ 5. *Travel* means "to go from one place to another place."

_____ 6. The Canada goose probably travels from north to south during the fall.

Use words in context.

Write one of the following words in each blank.

loud   migratory   noise   travels

A _____ bird _____ in spring and fall.

The Canada goose makes a _____ _____ when it flies.

Check your comprehension.

Your teacher will ask you some questions about the information. Write the answers on the following lines.

1. _____.
2. _____.
3. _____.
4. _____.

Listen to the information again. Check your answers while you listen.

Reading

Read for the main ideas.

Read the passage once quickly. Then write short answers to the following questions.

1. What kind of bird is the Canada goose?

2. How big is it?

3. What is its main color?

4. Does it live around water?

Underline key words and phrases.

Read the passage again. This time, underline the words that answer the preceding questions.

Canada Goose

The Canada goose is a migratory bird of North America. It spends summers in Canada and Alaska. When fall comes, it flies south to the central and southern parts of the United States and to northern Mexico. It travels in large flocks, flying in V formation. It makes a honking noise while it is flying.

The adult goose varies in size from 63 to 108 centimeters long. It is mostly gray; its head, neck, and tail are black. It has white patches on the two sides of its face.

The Canada goose lives around marshes, lakes, ponds, and fields. Like other geese, it eats grasses, seeds, and aquatic plants.

Use words in context.

Look at the following pairs of sentences. Write one word in each blank to make the second sentence of each pair mean the same as the first sentence. You will find the words you need in the reading about the Canada goose.

1. Some Canada geese stay in the middle part of the United States during the winter.
   Canada geese _____ the winter in the _____
   _____ part of the United States.

2. Canada geese live by water.
   Canada geese live _____ water.

Write one word in each blank. Find the words in the reading passage.

The size of the geese _____. Some are 63 centimeters long; others are 108 centimeters long.

They fly together with other Canada geese. They fly in

_____.

Find specific information.

Answer the following questions.

1. What is a migratory bird?
   a. a bird that lives in the same place all year
   b. a bird that lives in one place during summer and another place during winter

2. Where does the Canada goose spend summers?

3. Where does it spend winters?

4. About how big is an adult goose?

5. What color is it?

6. What kinds of places does it live in?

7. What does it eat?

8. Does it travel alone, or does it travel in a flock?

9. It is quiet when it flies?

Use information to make guesses.

1. Which does the Canada goose prefer—cool weather or hot weather?
2. Is the Canada goose a waterfowl?

Summarize the reading.

Complete the following sentences. Do this exercise two times. Do it orally the first time; do it in writing the second time.

(1) The Canada goose is a migratory. . . . (2) It spends summer in. . . .
(3) It spends winter in. . . . (4) The adult goose varies in size from. . . .
(5) It is mostly. . . . (6) It lives around. . . . (7) It eats. . . .

Discuss birds and animals.

What are some unusual birds or animals in your country? Some animals, like birds, migrate. Can you think of some?

Part Four

Outside Reading

Find information about a bird.

Go to the library. Find a book about birds. Look up one bird of your choice. Find the following information about the bird.

1. Name:
2. Size:
3. Color(s):
4. Place where it lives (habitat):

Lesson 5

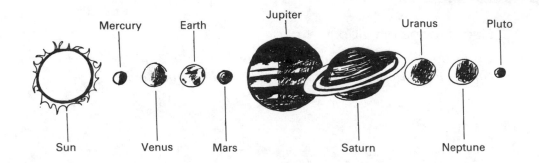

Mercury · Earth · Jupiter · Uranus · Pluto · Sun · Venus · Mars · Saturn · Neptune

Part One — SOLAR SYSTEM

Listening

Listen for the main idea.

Your teacher will give you some information. Listen to the information. Then choose the sentence which best tells what the information is about.

a. The information tells about the solar system.
b. The information tells about the sun.
c. The information discusses two ways planets in the solar system move.

Listen for words.

Fill in the blanks while listening to the information again. Use the following words, numbers, and expressions one or more times.

planet	rotate	9.8
planets	rotation	12
revolution		24
revolve		365

All the _____ in the solar system do two

things: They _____ around the sun, and they

_____, or turn, on their axes. The time it takes for one

_____ or for one _____ is different for

each _____. The earth, for example, makes one

_____ every _____ days and one

_____ every _____ hours. Jupiter, on the

other hand, makes one _____ every _____

earth years and one _____ every _____

earth hours.

Guess the meanings of words.

*Read the information. Then read the statements following the information. Put **T** in front of statements that are true. Put **F** in front of statements that are false.*

The earth is a planet. It revolves, or goes around, the sun, which is a star. The time it takes for the earth to make one revolution is called a year. The earth also rotates, or turns around and around. The time it takes for one rotation is called one day

_____ 1. *Revolve* means "go around."

_____ 2. *Rotate* and *revolve* have the same meaning.

_____ 3. A planet revolves around a star.

_____ 4. One earth rotation is 24 hours.

_____ 5. One earth revolution is equal to one day.

Use words in context.

Write one word in each blank.

day	revolve	rotate
planets	rotation	year
revolution		

The _____ _____ around the sun.

One _____ equals one _____. Planets also

_____ on their axes. One _____ equals

one _____.

Check your comprehension.

Your teacher will ask you some questions about the information. Listen to the questions. Then fill in the blanks with the correct answers.

1. All planets _____ around _____ and

_____ on their axes.

2. _____.

3. The earth revolves once every _____.

4. The earth rotates once every _____.

5. Jupiter revolves once every _____ earth years.

6. Jupiter rotates once every _____ earth hours.

Listen to the information again. Check your answers while you listen.

Reading

Preview the reading.

Look at the chart. List the four types of information it gives about the planets.

a. _____   c. _____

b. _____   d. _____

SOLAR SYSTEM

BODIES IN SOLAR SYSTEM	DISTANCE FROM THE SUN (millions of miles)	DIAMETER (thousands of miles)	PERIOD OF REVOLUTION (earth days)	PERIOD OF ROTATION (earth hours)
Sun	—	856.0	—	648.0
Planets				
Mercury	36	3.0	88	1,416.0
Venus	67	7.8	225	5,832.0
Earth	93	7.9	365	24.0
Mars	142	4.2	687	24.6
Jupiter	483	89.0	4,380	9.8
Saturn	887	75.0	10,585	10.3
Uranus	1,784	31.0	30,660	10.8
Neptune	2,797	28.0	60,225	15.7
Pluto	3,672	4.0	90,520	144.0

Find specific information.

1. How many bodies (sun and planets) are in the solar system?

2. How many planets are listed in the chart?

3. Which planet
   a. is closest to the sun?
   b. is farthest from the sun?
   c. is the largest?
   d. is the smallest?
   e. has the longest year?
   f. has the shortest year?
   g. has the longest day?
   h. has the shortest day?

Use the information to make guesses.

*Put **T** in front of statements that are true. Put **F** in front of statements that are false.*

_____ 1. Planets that are farther from the sun take a longer time to make one revolution.

_____ 2. Planets that are farther from the sun take a longer time to make one rotation.

_____ 3. Planets with larger diameters take a longer time to make one rotation.

Write the answer to the following question.

4. Suppose scientists discovered a new planet 118 million miles from the sun. About how many days do you think it would take the new planet to revolve one time around the sun?

Use words in context.

Write one of the following words or expressions in each blank.

days	revolves
diameter	rotates
hours	solar system
planets	million

The earth is one of nine _____ in the

_____. It is 93 _____ miles from

the sun. It _____ around the sun once every 365

_____. It _____ once on its axis every 24

_____. Its _____ is 7.9 thousand miles.

Recall the information.

Try to talk or write about the solar system and the earth without looking back at the chart or previous exercises. Use the following list as a guide.

solar system — nine planets
planet   — closest to the sun
                farthest from the sun
                largest
                smallest
earth   — distance from the sun
                revolves
                rotates

Part Two — SPACE BUBBLES

Listening

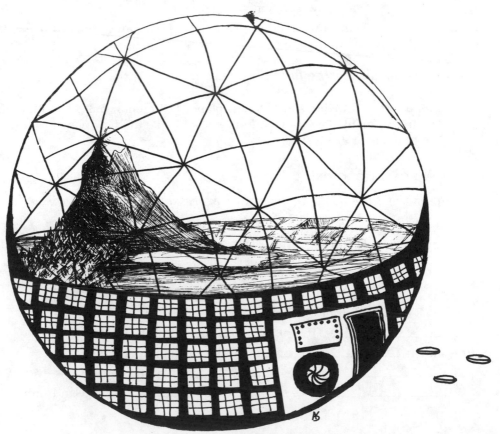

Listen for the main idea.

Your teacher will give you some information. Listen to the information. Then choose the sentence which best tells what the information is about.

a. We may have to control population on the earth someday because the earth will be too crowded.
b. Birth control is the best way to control population.
c. People must live in space someday.

Listen for words.

Fill in the blanks while listening to the information again. Use the following words and expressions.

birth control   overpopulated
control the population   practice
enough   space
millions

The earth might become _____ one day If that happens, there will be too many people, and there won't be

_____ food for people to eat. _____ of people might die. We must not let that happen. We have to think of ways to

_____. Perhaps everyone should _____

_____. Or perhaps some people should leave earth and go to live in _____.

Guess the meanings of words.

*Read the information. Then read the statements following the information. Put **T** in front of statements that are true. Put **F** in front of statements that are false.*

When there are too many people in a country, for example, we say that the country is overpopulated.

_____   1.   *Overpopulated* means too many people.

When people do not want more children, they practice birth control.

_____   2.   People practice birth control when they want to stop having children.

When people do not have enough food to eat, they might die or starve to death.

_____ 3. People starve to death by eating too much food.

Use words in context.

Write one of the following words or phrases in each blank.

birth control   overpopulated   starve

1. The earth may have too many people one day. It may become _____.

2. Millions of people may _____ because they don't have enough food to eat.

3. People need to practice _____ so that they have fewer children.

Check your comprehension.

Your teacher will ask you some questions about the information. Listen to the questions. Then answer the questions by filling in the blanks.

1. People might _____.
2. Everyone can practice _____.
3. People should leave _____ and live in _____.

Listen to the information again. Check your answers while you listen.

Reading

Read for the main ideas.

Read the story quickly. Then answer the following questions.

1. What does Max live in?

2. Where is it?

3. Why are Max and the other people living there?

4. Does Max like living there?

5. Does Max's grandfather like living there?

Bubbles in Space

My name is Max. I live in a large bubble (a space station). It is about 200 miles in diameter, and it travels around in space. My bubble and a million other bubbles like it were launched from the earth about 70 years ago.

I was born here. It is the only world I know. But my grandfather, who is 90, came from the earth. In fact, he helped build this bubble.

The earth was overpopulated then, and people were starving to death. Leaders from countries around the world had a meeting to solve the problem of overpopulation. They decided to send one billion people into space to live in bubbles. They also decided to force people who remained on earth to practice birth control. From that time, no family could have more than one child.

A computer selected the people who had to leave the earth. These people came from every nation. Each person could choose to be in a bubble with people who were of the same race, culture, and language. Or, as my grandfather did, they could select a bubble with people from various races, cultures, and languages.

We grow or make everything we need. We have grass, trees, flowers, birds, and even a small mountain. Of course, the mountain is artificial, and so is our weather, which does not change from day to day. We never have bad weather.

There are almost 2,000 of us living in my bubble. We live the same kind of life that people on the earth do. We do the same kinds of things.

This bubble is home to me. My grandfather, however, remembers the earth, where he was born. Sometimes he wants to be able to climb real mountains, fly long distances in airplanes, or experience changes in weather. He says that he wants to go back to the earth, to die and to be buried there.

Of course, my grandfather can't return to the earth. This bubble has been drifting in space for 70 years. It is very far from the earth.

Decide when the events happened.

Circle the letter in front of the correct answer.

1. This story happens in the
   a. present.
   b. future.

2. Max's grandfather left earth in the
   a. past.
   b. future.

3. The earth is overpopulated in the

    a. present.

    b. future.

Put events in the proper order.

Study the events listed below. Decide when each of the events happened. Then order the events according to when they happened. 1 has been entered in front of the event that happened first. Now write 2 in front of the event that happened second, and so on.

_____ Bubble was launched.

_____ Max was born.

_____ Bubble was built.

_____ Leaders decided some people had to leave the earth.

_____ Max wrote this story.

__1__ Max's grandfather was born on the earth.

Guess the meanings of words.

Read each section of the story. Then circle the letter in front of the answers you think are correct. Try not to use a dictionary.

My name is Max. I live in a large bubble. It is about 200 miles in diameter, and it travels around in space. My bubble and a million other bubbles like it were launched from the earth about 70 years ago.

1. *Launch* means

    a. to keep something on earth.

    b. to send something away from earth.

2. *Space* means

    a. a place away from earth.

    b. a place on earth.

Leaders from countries around the world had a meeting to solve the problem of overpopulation. They decided to send one billion people into space to live in bubbles. They also decided to force people who remained on earth to practice birth control. From that time, no family could have more than one child.

3. *Solve a problem* means

    a. to forget about the problem.

    b. to find an answer to the problem.

4. When we say that the leaders decided to *force* people to practice birth control, we mean that

   a. they decided that people could practice birth control if they wanted to.
   b. they decided that people must practice birth control.

A computer selected the people who had to leave the earth. These people came from every nation. Each person could choose to be in a bubble with people who were of the same race, culture, and language. Or, as my grandfather did, they could select a bubble with people from various races, cultures, and languages.

5. *Choose* and *select*

   a. have about the same meaning.
   b. have very different meanings.

We grow or make everything we need. We have grass, trees, flowers, birds, and even a small mountain. Of course, the mountain is artificial, and so is our weather, which does not change from day to day. We never have bad weather.
   . . . This bubble is home to me. My grandfather, however, remembers the earth, where he was born. Sometimes he wants to be able to climb real mountains, fly long distances in airplanes, or experience changes in weather. He says that he wants to go back to the earth, to die and to be buried there.

6. Something *artificial*

   a. is made by humans.
   b. is not made by humans—is natural.

7. *Artificial* and *real*

   a. have opposite meanings.
   b. have the same meaning.

Of course, my grandfather can't return to the earth. This bubble has been drifting in space for 70 years. It is very far from the earth.

8. Drifting means

   a. moving.
   b. not moving.

Use words in context.

Write one word or expression in each blank.

diameter   drifting   launched   space

The bubble has a _____ of 200 miles. It has been
_____ in _____ since it was
_____ from earth about 70 years ago.

choose (2)   overpopulated   selected   solve the problem

The earth was _____. Leaders from many nations decided
to _____ by having a billion people live in bubbles in space.
A computer _____ those who had to leave the earth.
People could _____ to be in a bubble with people who
were like them, or they could _____ a bubble that had
many people who were different from them.

artificial   life   live

Grass, trees, flowers, birds, and a small _____ mountain are
in the bubble. People _____ the same kind of
_____ people on earth do.

experience   real

Max's grandfather remembers the earth. He wants to climb
_____ mountains, fly in airplanes, and
_____ changes in the weather.

Check your comprehension.

*Read each section of the story. Then read the statements that follow each
section. Put **T** in front of each statement that is true. Put **F** in front of
each statement that is false.*

Bubbles in Space

My name is Max. I live in a large bubble (space station). It is
about 200 miles in diameter, and it travels around in space. My bubble
and a million other bubbles like it were launched from the earth about
70 years ago.

_____ 1. The bubble is large.

_____ 2. There is only one bubble.

_____ 3. The bubble is not new.

I was born here. It is the only world I know. But my grandfather, who is now 90, came from the earth. In fact, he helped build this bubble.

_____ 4. Max came from the earth.

_____ 5. Max's grandfather came from the earth.

_____ 6. Max's grandfather was an old man when he helped build the bubble.

The earth was overpopulated then, and people were starving to death.

_____ 7. People had to leave the earth because it was destroyed.

_____ 8. People left the earth because there were too many people there.

Leaders from countries around the world had a meeting to solve the problem of overpopulation. They decided to send one billion people into space to live in bubbles. They also decided to force people who remained on earth to practice birth control. From that time, no family could have more than one child.

_____ 9. The leaders decided to do two things to control the population of the earth.

_____ 10. The leaders said that people could have many children.

_____ 11. A small number of people left the earth.

A computer selected the people who had to leave the earth. These people came from every nation. Each person could choose to be in a bubble with people who were of the same race, culture, and language. Or, as my grandfather did, they could select a bubble with people from various races, cultures, and languages.

_____ 12. The people who had to live in bubbles were chosen by computer.

_____ 13. People could choose to live in a bubble or to stay on earth.

_____ 14. People could choose to be with people who were like them.

_____ 15. People could choose to be with people who were different from them.

We grow or make everything we need. We have grass, trees, flowers, birds, and even a small mountain. Of course, the mountain is artificial, and so is our weather, which does not change from day to day. We never have bad weather.

There are nearly 2,000 of us now living in my bubble. We live the same kind of life that people on earth do. We do the same kinds of things.

_____ 16.   The weather is seldom the same.

_____ 17.   The daily life of the people in the bubble is probably very different from the daily life of the people on earth.

This bubble is home to me. My grandfather, however, remembers the earth, where he was born. Sometimes he wants to be able to climb real mountains, fly long distances in airplanes, or to experience changes in weather. He says that he wants to go back to the earth, to die and be buried there.

Of course, my grandfather can't return to the earth. This bubble has been drifting in space for 70 years. It is very far from earth.

_____ 18.   Max and his grandfather have different feelings about living in the bubble.

_____ 19.   They have the same feelings about living on earth.

_____ 20.   Max's grandfather wants to live on earth again.

_____ 21.   Max's grandfather will live on earth again.

Use information to make guesses.

Read the information. Then try to answer the question that follows the information.

My bubble and a million other bubbles like it were launched from the earth about 70 years ago.

. . . Leaders from countries around the world had a meeting to solve the problem of overpopulation. They decided to send one billion people into space to live in bubbles.

How many people were put into each bubble?

*Write **M** in front of the sentences that tell you that Max probably likes the bubble. Put **G** in front of the sentences that tell you that Max's grandfather probably does not like the bubble.*

_____ 1.   This bubble is home to me.

_____ 2.   Sometimes he wants to be able to climb real mountains, fly long distances in airplanes, or experience changes in weather.

————————   3. He says that he wants to go back to the earth, to die and to be buried there.

————————   4. I was born here. It is the only world I know.

Determine the meanings of pronouns.

Write a **noun** *in each blank. The noun must have the same meaning as the word just before the parenthesis.*

My name is Max. I (————————————————) live in a large bubble. . . .

I was born here (————————————————). It (————————————————) is the only world I know. But my grandfather, who is 90, came from the earth. In fact, he (————————————————) helped build this bubble. . . .

. . . Leaders from countries around the world had a meeting to solve the problem of overpopulation. They (————————————————) decided to send one billion people into space to live in bubbles. They (————————————————) also decided to force people who remained on earth to practice birth control.

. . . This bubble is home to me (————————————————). My grandfather, however, remembers the earth, where he (————————————————) was born. Sometimes he (————————————————) wants to be able to climb real mountains, fly long distances in airplanes, or experience changes in weather. He says that he (————————————————) wants to go back to the earth, to die and be buried there (————————————————).

Of course, my grandfather can't return to the earth. This bubble has been drifting in space for 70 years. It (————————————————) is very far from the earth.

Summarize the reading.

Complete the following sentences. Do this exercise twice. Do it orally the first time. Do it in writing the second time.

Max lives in a bubble. The bubble was put . . . 70 years ago. The earth was. . . . One billion people . . . and live in space bubbles. Life in the bubbles is like. . . . There are. . . . The bubble is . . . to Max, but his grandfather. . . . He wants . . . but he can't. The bubble is. . . .

Give your opinion.

Which would you prefer, to be in a bubble with people of various races, cultures, and languages, or to be in a bubble with people of the same race, culture, and language? Why?

Part Three — SPACE EXPLORATION

Listening

Listen for the main idea.

Your teacher will give you some information. Listen to the information. Then choose the sentence that best tells what the information is about.

a. The information tells about the solar system.

b. The information discusses the history of space exploration.

c. The information is about the Soviet exploration of the universe.

Listen for words.

Fill in the blanks while listening to the information again. Use the following words and expressions.

back-and-forth	solar system
explore	space
orbit	space age
planets	space shuttle
satellite(s)	space stations

The space age began in 1957 when the Soviets sent a _____ called Sputnik 1 into _____ around the earth. Since then, people have walked on the moon, lived for long periods of time in _____, and used a _____ _____ to travel _____ between earth and _____. Also, _____ have been sent to _____ _____ — _____ in the _____ _____.

Guess the meanings of words.

Read the information. Then read the statements following the informa tion. Circle the letter in front of the correct answers.

The first space shuttle, Columbia, went into space and came back to earth five times. It made five flights back-and-forth between earth and space.

1. *Back-and-forth* means

   a. to go somewhere and return a number of times.
   b. to come back many times.

Sputnik 1 was the first object to be put into space. The satellite was put into orbit around the earth on October 4, 1957.

2. A *satellite* is

   a. an object on the earth.
   b. an object that people put into space.

3. *Orbit* means

   a. to go around something.
   b. to go into space.

Scientists have sent satellites to explore planets in the solar system. Therefore, we know a lot about the planets today.

4. *Explore* means
   a. to travel to many places.
   b. to go someplace in order to learn about it.

Use words in context.

Write one word or expression in each blank.

back-and-forth   orbit   satellites

The space shuttle goes _____ between earth and space. It does many things while it is in space. Sometimes, it puts _____ into _____ around the earth.

Check your comprehension.

Your teacher will ask you some questions about the information. Listen to the questions. Then answer the questions by filling in the blanks.

1. It began in _____.
2. The Russians sent _____.
3. a. People have walked _____.
   b. A space shuttle has traveled back-and-forth between _____ and _____.
   c. Satellites have been sent to explore _____.

Listen to the information again. Check your answers while you listen.

Reading

Preview the reading.

Read the information quickly. Look for the years in which the following events happened.

1. The first satellite was placed into orbit in _____.
2. The first human went into space in _____.
3. The Gemini program began in _____.
4. People landed on the moon in _____.
5. The first space shuttle was launched in _____.

*Putting People into Space**

The space age began on October 4, 1957, with the successful orbiting of the earth by the Soviet satellite, Sputnik 1. Since that time, the United States has been making serious efforts to put people into space.

The first manned space program of the United States was Project Mercury. The goal of this program, which was to put an American into space, was achieved on May 5, 1961, when Alan Shepherd went on a suborbital flight that lasted 15 minutes and 28 seconds.

The Gemini program began in 1965. Its purpose was to study the effects of long periods of spaceflight on humans.

Apollo, the name given to the program to put an American on the moon, followed the Gemini program. The goal of this program was achieved on July 20, 1969, when Neil A. Armstrong and Edwin E. Aldrin, Jr. climbed out of their spaceship and walked on the moon.

The next program, Project Skylab, resulted in America's first earth-orbiting space station. The purpose of this program was to demonstrate that people can work and live in space for long periods of time.

After Apollo and Project Skylab, America started the space shuttle program. This space transportation system was developed to reduce the cost of using space for commercial, scientific, and defense purposes. The first space shuttle flight was made on April 12, 1981. This shuttle program continues into the 1990s.

Guess the meanings of words.

Read each section of the information. Circle the letter in front of the answer that you think is correct.

The space age began on October 4, 1957, with the successful orbiting of the earth by the Soviet satellite, Sputnik 1.

1. *Successful orbiting* means that
   a. Sputnik 1 was able to orbit the earth.
   b. Sputnik 1 was not able to orbit the earth.

Since that time, the United States has been making serious efforts to put people into space.

2. *Serious efforts* means that
   a. after Sputnik 1, the United States tried hard to put people in space.
   b. after Sputnik 1, the United States did not try to put people in space.

*Adapted from *U.S. Space Goals Came about Due to Soviet Efforts*. Tom Scott, *Houston Chronicle*, February 3, 1986. Reproduced by permission of publisher.

The first manned space program of the United States was Project Mercury. The goal of this program, which was to put an American into space. . . .

3. *Manned space program* means

    a. to put people into space.
    b. to put animals into space.

4. *Goal* means

    a. something that you want to do.
    b. something that you do not want to do.

The goal of this program, which was to put an American into space, was achieved on May 5, 1961, when Alan Shepherd went on a suborbital flight that lasted 15 minutes and 28 seconds.

5. *Achieve a goal* means that

    a. you are able to do what you wanted to do.
    b. you are not able to do what you wanted to do.

6. *Sub* means "under." Therefore, in a *suborbital flight*, a spacecraft

    a. goes high enough above the earth to go into orbit.
    b. goes very high above the earth, but not high enough to go into orbit.

The Gemini program began in 1965. Its purpose was to study the effects of long periods of spaceflight on humans.

7. The meaning of *purpose*

    a. is very different from the meaning of *goal*.
    b. is about the same as the meaning of *goal*.

The next program, Project Skylab, resulted in America's first earth-orbiting space station. The purpose of this program was to demonstrate that people can work and live in space for long periods of time.

8. *Demonstrate*, as it is used here, means

    a. to show that people can work and live in space for long periods of time.
    b. not to show that people can work and live in space for long periods of time.

9. *Resulted in* means that

    a. the space station was built because of Project Skylab.
    b. Project Skylab was started because of the space station.

After Apollo and Project Skylab, America started the space shuttle program. This space transportation system was developed to reduce the cost of using space for commercial, scientific, and defense purposes.

10. *Reduce the cost* means that
   a. the shuttle program was developed to increase the cost of using space for commercial, scientific, and defense purposes.
   b. the shuttle program was developed to lower the cost of using space for commercial, scientific, and defense purposes.

11. *Developed* means
   a. to begin something and then to make it better.
   b. to begin something.

12. *Commercial* means
   a. scientific.
   b. business.

13. *Defense purposes* means
   a. the same as *military purposes*.
   b. the same as *commercial purposes*.

Find specific information.

Answer questions 1 through 3 and do exercise 4 filling out the chart on next page.

1. When did the first satellite go into orbit? What country put it into orbit?

2. Who was the first astronaut? What country did he come from?

3. What country was Neil Armstrong from? What did he do? When?

4. Outline the U.S.'s manned space program by filling in the following chart. You will find information you need in the reading. However, not all information is in the reading; therefore, you will not be able to fill in the chart completely.

UNITED STATES SPACE PROGRAM, 1961 to 1985

APPROXIMATE YEARS	PROGRAM NAME	ASTRONAUTS NAMED (if any)	PURPOSE, ACCOMPLISHMENT, AND DATE
Late 1950s, early 1960s	Project Mercury	Alan Shepherd	Suborbital flight on May 5, 1961

Give your opinion.

Space programs are very expensive. They use money that could be used for other things. How do you feel about that? Should we spend a lot of money on space programs? Why, or why not?

Part Four

Outside Reading

Determine the population of the earth.

Look up earth *or* world *in an encyclopedia. Try to find out what the population of the earth is now.*

Learn about an astronaut.

Look up space *or* U.S. space program *in an encyclopedia. Find the name of one astronaut. Find out something interesting about that astronaut. Share your information with your classmates.*

Lesson 6

Part One — MAJOR LANGUAGES

Listening

Listen for tne main idea.

Your teacher will give you some information. Listen to the information. Then choose the answer which best tells what the information is about.

a. speakers of Chinese
b. number of languages in the world
c. people who study languages

Listen for words.

Fill in the blanks while listening to the information again. Use the following words and expressions.

different (2)	linguists
eight	major (2)
estimate	thirteen
four	three
	three-quarters

We do not know how many _____ languages there are in the world. _____, people who study language as a science, _____ that there are from _____ or _____ thousand to about _____ thousand _____ languages. If we count only _____ languages, however, the number is much smaller. In fact, only _____ _____ languages are spoken by _____ of the people in the world.

Guess the meanings of words.

*Read the information. Then read the statements following the information. Put **T** in front of the statements that are true. Put **F** in front of the statements that are false.*

There are many languages in the world. Some major languages have several hundred million speakers. Some other languages may have only several thousand speakers. Of course, scientists do not know exactly how many people speak a language. They must estimate the number of speakers.

_____ 1. A major language has a very large number of speakers.

_____ 2. *Major* and *small* have similar meanings.

_____ 3. We know exactly when we estimate.

_____ 4. *Estimate* and *guess* have similar meanings.

Check your comprehension.

Your teacher will ask you some questions about the information. Listen to the questions. Then write out the answers.

1. _____.

2. _____.

3. _____.

4. A linguist is a person who _____ as a _____.

Listen to the information again. Check your answers while you listen.

Reading

Preview the reading.

Look at the chart. What information does it give?

a. _____ .

b. _____ .

MAJOR LANGUAGES OF THE WORLD

	Numbers in millions
Italian	65
Indonesian	80
French	85
Bengali	100
Portuguese	105
Japanese	110
German	120
Arabic	130
Spanish	205
English	400
Chinese	800

Thousands of languages are spoken around the world. Many of these languages are spoken in just one part of the world and have a relatively small number of speakers. The chart shows the 11 languages that have the most speakers. Note that Chinese is the language with the most speakers. It is, however, spoken mostly by people living in one country—China. English has only about half as many speakers as Chinese, but it is spoken in more areas of the world. In fact, English is the native language of people in five different countries: Australia, Canada, Great Britain, New Zealand, and the United States. In addition, English is spoken as a second language by millions of people living around the world.

Find specific information.

Study the chart, write out answers to the questions.

1. Which of the languages in the chart has the most speakers?
   Which language has the fewest speakers?

2. Which language in the chart is probably spoken in most areas?

3. Eleven languages are shown in the chart. Are there many more languages
   that are not listed?

Use information to make guesses.

1. Japanese is an example of a language that is spoken primarily in only one
   country. Therefore, you can guess the approximate population of Japan
   from the information in the chart. Write your answer below.

   Japan ————————————————

2. If a person takes a trip around the world, which language will he or she want
   to be able to speak?

Discuss languages spoken in your country.

Is more than one language commonly spoken in your country? What are those
languages? About what percentage of the population speaks each of those
languages?

Part Two — STRANGE ENGLISH

Listening

Listen for the main idea.

*Your teacher will give you some information. Listen to the information.
Then choose the answer that best tells what the information is about.*

a. What happens when you never speak your native language again?

b. What happens when you are living in another country for a long time?

c. What happens if you do not speak your native language for a long time?

Listen for words.

Fill in the blanks while listening to the information again. Use the following words and expressions:

after	long	native
begin	mispronounce	slowly
forget		

What happens if you speak only a foreign language for a
_____ time? Will you _____ your
_____ language? Probably not, but you might have some
problems when you first _____ speaking your
_____ language again. For example, you might speak too
_____, _____ some words, have trouble
finding the right words, or make grammatical errors. But do not worry.
_____ you speak your _____ language
again, these problems go away.

Find opposite words.

Write one word in each blank.

after	long	right
begin	mispronounce	slow
forget	native	

Opposite Word

before   _____

end   _____

fast   _____

foreign   _____

pronounce   _____

remember   _____

short   _____

wrong   _____

Check your comprehension.

Your teacher will ask you some questions about the information. Listen to the questions. Then write down the answers.

1. _____.
2. _____.
3. _____.

Listen to the information again. Check your answers while you listen.

Reading

Read for the main ideas.

Read the story quickly. Then write out answers to the following questions.

1. How did the writer of this story travel from Japan to the United States? (See paragraph 3.)

2. What language did the writer speak while traveling? (See paragraph 3.)

3. What trouble did the writer have at the hotel? (See paragraph 5.)

Mister! You Speak Strange English

Will you forget your native language if you speak only a foreign language for a long time?

I don't think so, but some amusing things can happen.

I sailed from Japan to the United States in March 1971. I didn't have much money, so I bought the cheapest ticket and shared a cabin with five young Japanese tourists who did not speak any English. In order to communicate with them, I had to speak Japanese during the entire trip.

The ship docked in San Francisco 14 days after it left Yokohama. After my Japanese roommates and I passed through customs and immigration, we went to a hotel where I helped them get a room.

Perhaps because I had been using only Japanese for such a long time, I had a lot of trouble speaking English at the hotel. I couldn't pronounce words correctly. I made grammar mistakes. I spoke too slowly because I had difficulty finding the right words.

Slightly embarrassed, I jokingly said to the desk clerk, "Excuse my bad English, please."

"Oh, don't apologize because of your English!" said the clerk, smiling nicely. "I think it is really good."

She did not realize I was joking. She thought I was a foreigner and that for a foreigner my English was really good.

I explained to her that I was born in the U.S., that I was a U.S. citizen, and that my native language was English.

She looked up, straight into my eyes. "You know, mister," she said seriously, "for an American your English is really bad!"

Guess the meanings of words.

*Read the information. Then read the statements that follow the information. Put **T** in front of each statement that is true. Put **F** in front of each statement that is false.*

I didn't have much money, so I bought the cheapest ticket and shared a cabin with five young Japanese tourists who did not speak any English. In order to communicate with them, I had to speak Japanese during the entire trip.

_____ 1. The cheapest ticket is the most expensive ticket.

_____ 2. The Japanese were tourists; therefore, they were going to the United States on business.

_____ 3. In this story, *communicate* and *speak* have about the same meaning.

_____ 4. He had to speak Japanese during all of the trip.

_____ 5. A cabin is a room on a ship.

_____ 6. When you share a cabin, you are the only person staying in it.

The ship docked in San Francisco 14 days after it left Yokohama. After my Japanese roommates and I passed through customs and immigration, we went to a hotel where I helped them get a room.

_____ 7. *To dock* means to "to go away" or "to leave."

_____ 8. *Pass through* means "to go through."

I had a lot of trouble speaking English at the hotel. I couldn't pronounce words correctly. I made grammar mistakes. I spoke too slowly because I had difficulty finding the right words.

_____ 9. *Trouble* and *difficulty* have very different meanings here.

_____ 10. The writer had difficulty pronouncing words.

Slightly embarrassed, I jokingly said to the desk clerk, "Excuse my bad English, please."

_____ 11. You feel bad when you are embarrassed.

_____ 12. *Slightly* means "a little."

_____ 13. The writer was embarrassed a lot.

_____ 14. The desk clerk was a person working at the hotel.

"Oh, don't apologize because of your English!" said the clerk, smiling nicely. "I think it is really good."
She did not realize I was joking.

_____ 15. You apologize when you say you are sorry or when you excuse yourself for something you did or said.

_____ 16. The clerk knew that the writer was joking.

_____ 17. *Realize* and *understand* have similar meanings.

Use words in context.

Write one word or expression in each blank.

cabin   cheapest   communicate   entire   shared   tourists

The writer traveled by ship to San Francisco. He bought the _____ ticket and _____ a _____ with five Japanese _____. The writer had to _____ in Japanese during the _____ trip.

apologize   embarrassed   native
desk clerk   jokingly   passed through
docked   mispronounced   realize
                                  trouble

The ship _____ in San Francisco 14 days later. They _____ customs and immigration and then went to a hotel. At the hotel, the writer became _____ when he had _____ speaking English and _____ words. _____, he told the _____ to excuse his English, but the clerk did not _____ he was joking and told him not to _____ for his English. The clerk did not know that the writer was not a _____ speaker of English.

Check your comprehension.

*Read each section of the story. Then read the statements that follow each section. Put **T** in front of statements that are true. Put **F** in front of statements that are false.*

Will you forget your native language if you speak only a foreign language for a long time?

I don't think so, but some amusing things can happen.

_____ 1. You will probably forget your native language.
_____ 2. You will not forget it, but you might have some trouble.

I sailed from Japan to the United States in March 1971. I didn't have much money, so I bought the cheapest ticket and shared a cabin with five young Japanese tourists who did not speak any English. In order to communicate with them, I had to speak Japanese during the entire trip

_____ 3. The writer was trying not to spend a lot of money.
_____ 4. The Japanese tourists bought the cheapest ticket.
_____ 5. The Japanese could speak English.
_____ 6. The writer could speak Japanese.

The ship docked in San Francisco 14 days after it left Yokohama. After my Japanese roommates and I passed through customs and immigration, we went to a hotel where I helped them get a room.

_____ 7. The trip from Yokohama to San Francisco took two weeks.
_____ 8. The writer helped the Japanese get a hotel room.
_____ 9. First, the writer and the Japanese traveled to San Francisco for 14 days. Second, the writer helped the Japanese get a hotel room. Third, they went through customs and immigration. Fourth, they went to a hotel.

Perhaps because I had been using only Japanese for such a long time, I had a lot of trouble speaking English at the hotel. I couldn't pronounce words correctly. I made grammar mistakes. I spoke too slowly because I had difficulty finding the right words.

_____ 10. The writer was not a native speaker of English.
_____ 11. The writer had difficulty speaking English.

Slightly embarrassed, I jokingly said to the desk clerk, "Excuse my bad English, please."

"Oh, don't apologize because of your English!" said the clerk, smiling nicely. "I think it is really good."

_____ 12. The writer made a joke because he was embarrassed.

_____ 13. The clerk thought the writer's English was very good.

She did not realize I was joking. She thought I was a foreigner and that for a foreigner my English was really good.

I explained to her that I was born in the U.S., that I was a U.S. citizen, and that my native language was English.

_____ 14. The clerk knew the writer was joking.

_____ 15. The clerk did not know the writer was a native speaker of English; therefore, she thought his English was good.

She looked up, straight into my eyes. "You know, mister," she said seriously, "for an American your English is really bad!"

_____ 16. After the clerk realized the writer was a native speaker of English, she thought his English was good.

_____ 17. The clerk thought the American's English was bad.

Use the information to make guesses.

Answer the following questions. Look in the story for clues to the correct answers.

1. Do you think the writer was young or old when this story happened? Why do you think so?

2. Do you think the writer enjoyed what happened in the hotel in San Francisco? Why, or why not?

Summarize the reading.

Complete the following sentences. Do this exercise two times. Do it orally the first time. Do it in writing the second time.

(1) The author traveled from . . . to . . . by. . . . (2) He shared a . . . with. . . . (3) He spoke. . . . (4) After the ship docked . . . he went with the Japanese to. . . . (5) At the . . . he had. . . . (6) He jokingly told the clerk. . . . (7) The clerk said. . . . (8) But after the clerk learned that he was . . . she said. . . .

Discuss communication problems.

Discuss a time when you had difficulty communicating in your native language or in a second language.

Part Three — **TYPES OF LANGUAGES**

Listening

Listen for the main idea.

Your teacher will give you some information. Listen to the information. Then choose the answer which best tells what the information is about.

a. You have to learn new grammatical rules when you learn a second language.

b. The way words become singular or plural is different in a second language.

c. When you learn a second language, you have to learn new grammatical rules and a new way of thinking.

Listen for words.

Fill in the blanks while listening to the information again. Use the following words and expressions.

culture	rules
native language	second language
reflects	thinking

Learning a _____ is not easy. First, the _____ of the language are different from the _____ of our _____. Second, the way of _____ in the _____ is different. Each language _____ a different _____ and, therefore, has a different way of looking at the world. We must learn a new _____ as well as new grammatical _____ when we learn a _____.

Guess the meanings of words.

*Read the information. Then read the statements that follow the information. Put **T** in front of statements that are true. Put **F** in front of statements that are false.*

John speaks two languages, English and Korean. He learned English when he was a child. He learned Korean after he finished college and went to live in Korea for a couple of years.

_____ 1. John's native language is Korean.
_____ 2. John's second language is Korean.

Different cultures have different kinds of food, different ways of acting, different ways of thinking, and different languages.

_____ 3. People who live in different countries and speak different languages have different cultures.
_____ 4. People who live in the same country and speak the same language probably have the same culture.
_____ 5. People who speak different languages and live in different places probably have the same culture.

Japanese people feel close to nature; therefore, their language has several different words for rain. Their language reflects their culture.

_____ 6. We learn about the culture of people when we learn their language.
_____ 7. It is possible to learn the language of a people without learning anything about their culture.
_____ 8. If we learn the language of a people, we learn much about how they think and act.

Use words in context.

Write one word or expression in each blank.

culture   native language
different   second language
grammatical rules

When you learn a _____, you learn

_____ that are _____ from the rules
of your _____. Also, you learn about a new

_____.

Check your comprehension.

Your teacher will ask you some questions about the information. Listen to the questions. Then write out answers to the questions.

1. _____.
2. _____.
3. _____.

Listen to the information again. Check your answers while you listen.

Reading

Preview the reading.

Read the information very quickly. Find the answers to the following questions.

1. What are three types of languages?
   a. _____
   b. _____
   c. _____

2. Does the reading describe each type of language?

Types of Languages

Linguists sometimes classify languages into three types: agglutinating, isolating, and inflecting.

English is an agglutinating language. It uses prefixes and suffixes to build new words. For example, the *ness* suffix in English changes adjectives to nouns (*sad*, *sadness*). The prefix *in* makes some words negative in meaning (*sufficient*, *insufficient*).

Vietnamese is an isolating language. It has almost no prefixes or suffixes. In Vietnamese nothing is added to verbs to show person, number, or tense. Also, nothing is added to nouns to show whether they are singular or plural.

Latin and Greek are inflectional languages. Words in Latin and Greek change their form when their grammatical function changes.

Some words in English are also inflectional. For example, the adjective *deep* changes to *depth* when it becomes a noun.

No language is completely isolating, agglutinating, or inflecting. However, classifying languages this way can help us understand major similarities and differences among the various languages of the world.

Guess the meanings of words.

Read the information. Then circle the letter in front of the correct answer.

Linguists sometimes classify languages into three types: isolating, agglutinating, and inflecting.

1. *Classify* means
   a. to put things into different groups.
   b. to put different things together into one group.

In Vietnamese, nothing is attached to verbs to show person, number, or tense. Also, nothing is added to nouns to show whether they are singular or plural.

2. *Attached* and *added*
   a. have the same meaning here.
   b. have different meanings here.

In inflectional languages, words change their form when their grammatical function in the sentence changes. An example of inflection in English is the adjective *deep*, which changes to *depth* when it becomes a noun.

3. The grammatical function of a word
   a. does not change when a word changes from an adjective to a noun.
   b. changes when a word changes from an adjective to a noun.

Find specific information.

Write out answers to the following questions.

1. Do words in isolating languages have prefixes and suffixes?
2. Do words in Vietnamese have prefixes and suffixes?
3. Do words in agglutinating languages have prefixes and suffixes?
4. Name a language that is an example of an agglutinating language.
5. Give an example of a prefix.

6. Give an example of a suffix.

7. What happens to words in inflecting languages when their grammatical function in a sentence changes?

8. Which is a better example of an inflecting language, Latin or English?

Outline the reading.

Fill in the blanks. The instructions on the left tell you what information to put in the blanks.

	Types of Languages
First type of language:	I. Agglutinating
Definition:	Prefixes and suffixes
Example language:	English
Second type of language:	II. _____
Definition:	Does not use ____ _____
	_____
Example language:	_____
Third type of language:	III. _____
Definition:	_____
Example language:	_____

Discuss your language.

Is your native language primarily isolating, agglutinating, or inflecting? Think of some examples and discuss them with your classmates.

Summarize the reading.

Complete the sentences. Do this exercise twice, once orally and again in writing.

The three types of languages are _____, _____, and _____. Isolating languages _____. Agglutinating languages,
(have/do not have prefixes and suffixes)
however, do have _____. Words in inflecting languages _____.

Part Four

Outside Reading

Find information about languages.

Make a list of all the different languages spoken by your classmates. Then, for each language, check an encyclopedia to see where the language is spoken and how many people speak it.

Lesson 7

Part One — BEARS

Listening

Listen for the main idea.

Your teacher will give you some information. Listen to the information. Then choose the sentence which best tells what the information is about.

a. enjoying national parks
b. seeing bears in national parks
c. camping and hiking in national parks

Listen for words.

Fill in the blanks while listening to the information again. Use the following words or expressions:

campers	hiking
campground	injure
camping	steal
damage	tents

Bears live in some of the national parks in the United States. Many people who go _____ and _____ in the parks hope to see a bear while they drive by car through a park or while they are _____ through the mountains. One place where people do not want to see a bear, however, is in the _____. Bears sometimes come into the _____ to _____ food from _____. When they do, they may _____ _____ or cars. However, they rarely _____ or kill people.

Guess the meanings of words.

*Read the information. Then read the statements following the information. Put **T** in front of statements that are true. Put **F** in front of statements that are false.*

Many people like to go camping in national parks. They put up tents in campgrounds and stay there for several days. During the day, many campers go hiking. When they return to the campground in the evening, they cook their dinner outside. Later they sit around a campfire for a while. They usually go to bed early in their tents because they are tired from walking all day.

_____   1. When people go camping, they sleep in tents.
_____   2. Tents are strong buildings.
_____   3. Campers are people.
_____   4. Campers do not like to be outdoors.
_____   5. A campground is a place where people put up tents.
_____   6. *Hiking* and *walking* have similar meanings.
_____   7. Campers sleep in tents.

Bears sometimes enter campgrounds and damage cars or tents when they try to steal food. On rare occasions, they injure campers who try to stop them from taking food. Fortunately, these attacks do not happen often. Camping is still very safe.

_____ 8. Campers do not want bears to steal food.
_____ 9. *To steal* means "to take something that is not yours."
_____ 10. *Rare occasions* means "almost never."
_____ 11. Someone who is injured might have to go to a hospital.
_____ 12. Things get injured; people get damaged.

Use words in context.

Write one word or expression in each blank.

campers   campground   camping   hiking   tent

John went _____ in Yellowstone National Park. He put up his _____ in a _____ and went _____ every day. At night, he sat around a fire and talked to other _____.

damage   injure   rare occasions   steal

On _____, bears may enter a campground to _____ food. When they do this, bears may _____ cars or tents. Very seldom do they _____ a camper.

Check your comprehension.

Your teacher will ask you some questions about the information. Listen to the questions. Then write out the answers to the questions.

1. _____.
2. _____.
3. They come to _____.
4. They may _____, or they may _____.

Listen to the information again. Check your answers while you listen.

Reading

Preview the reading.

Look at the chart. Then answer the following questions.

1. What is the chart about?

2. Where was the information gathered?

3. What years are covered in the chart?

BEAR ATTACKS IN YOSEMITE NATIONAL PARK, 1966–1976

YEAR	NUMBER OF VISITORS	NUMBER OF BEAR ATTACKS	DAMAGE IN $	NUMBER OF INJURIES	NUMBER OF VISITORS PER INJURY
1966	1,817,000	49	1,888	29	63,000
1967	2,201,500	72	2,843	11	200,000
1968	2,281,100	49	2,670	6	380,000
1969	2,291,300	86	6,360	12	191,000
1970	2,277,200	27	4,730	3	759,000
1971	2,416,400	103	11,835	10	242,000
1972	2,266,600	262	28,588	3	746,000
1973	2,339,400	246	26,367	16	146,000
1974	2,343,100	613	80,242	28	84,000
1975	2,619,000	975	113,197	15	175,000
1976	2,753,100	688	66,294	12	229,000
Avg.	2,327,791	288	31,365	13	292,273

Adapted from *Black Bear Management in Yosemite National Park*. Dale R. Harms. Paper presented at the Fourth International Conference on Bear Research and Management. Kalispell, Montana, 1977. Reproduced by permission of International Association of Bear Research and Management, Calgary, Canada.

Find specific information.

Look at the chart. Write out answers to the following questions.

1. How many people visited Yosemite National Park in 1970?

2. How many bear attacks were there in 1970?

3. What is the dollar amount of damage caused by bears to tents, cars, etc. in 1970?

4. Was this an increase or a decrease in cost over the previous year?

5. How many people were injured?

6. How many visitors were there per injury?

7. Fill in the blanks with the appropriate year.

Most visitors   _____

Most bear attacks   _____

Greatest damage ($)   _____

Most injuries   _____

8. Describe general trends from 1966 to 1976.

Number of visitors:
a. increased   c. remained the same
b. decreased   d. varied

Number of bear attacks:
a. increased   c. remained the same
b. decreased   d. varied

Cost:
a. increased   c. remained the same
b. decreased   d. varied

Number of injuries:
a. increased   c. remained the same
b. decreased   d. varied

Number of visitors per injury:
a. increased   c. remained the same
b. decreased   d. varied

Use information to make guesses.

Look at the chart. Then guess the answers to the following questions.

1. Over the years, the number of incidents has generally increased. Why?

2. In general, do you think it was safe for a person to visit Yosemite National Park from 1966 through 1976?

Summarize the chart.

Make generalizations based on the information in the chart. Write one word in each blank:

increased (2)   visitors

The number of bear attacks has _____ as the

number of _____ to the park has _____.

injuries   varied

The number of _____ per visitor has _____

greatly over the years.

injury   number   safe   visit

Generally speaking, it is _____ to

_____ the park because the _____ of

visitors per _____ is very high.

Part Two — SUSPENSE ON A MOUNTAIN TRAIL

Listening

Listen for the main idea.

Your teacher will give you some information. Listen to the information. Then choose the sentence which best tells what the information is about.

a. what to do if you meet a bear
b. hiking in the mountains and forest
c. the best places to go hiking in the mountains

Listen for words.

Fill in the blanks while listening to the information again. Use the following words and expressions:

afraid	move
attack	run away
experts	stand still
frighten	wait
go away	

What should you do if you meet a bear in the mountains or the forest?

1. _____ quickly.
2. Run toward the bear and try to _____ it away.
3. _____ and _____ for the bear to _____.

According to _____, you should stand where you are and not _____. If you _____, the bear may become frightened and _____ you. If you don't _____, the bear will probably _____. Bears are _____ of people. They will _____ if they can.

Guess the meanings of words.

*Read the information. Then read the statements that follow the information. Put **T** in front of statements that are true. Put **F** in front of statements that are false.*

Bear experts say that if you move, the bear will think you are going to injure it, and it may attack you. Therefore, they say that you should stand still. If you don't move, experts say, the bear will probably go away.

_____ 1. A bear expert is a person who does not know anything about bears.

_____ 2. *Stand still* and *move* have the same meaning here.

_____ 3. A bear comes toward you when it attacks.

Check your comprehension.

Your teacher will ask you some questions about the information. Listen to the questions. Then write out the answers to the questions.

1. _____.
2. _____.
3. _____.

Listen to the information again. Check your answers while you listen.

Reading

Find the main ideas.

Look through the story quickly. Write out answers to the following questions.

1. The author climbed up a mountain to see something one day. What did he go to see?

2. What did he meet on the trail when he was coming down?

Suspense on the Mountain Trail

One day I was hiking in the Mission Mountains of Montana and came to a large lake which was surrounded by big rocks and tall pine trees. The lake was formed by a stream which ran down from the mountains.

Someone told me that I could see a beautiful waterfall if I climbed upstream for about 30 minutes, and so I did.

The waterfall was indeed very beautiful. Water fell into a clear pool of cool water from a rock about 100 feet above.

I sat on a rock near the pool and ate some sandwiches I had brought with me. Some mountain climbers walked by; each of them greeted me with a "hello" or a "hi."

After I finished my lunch, I began to walk slowly back down the trail to the lake. Suddenly, I heard a noise and looked up. Fifty feet in front of me was a big, black bear. It had just come out of the trees and was standing in the trail.

"Don't move," I told myself. I stood there and stared at the bear. I never moved my eyes. My heart began to beat faster and faster.

The bear didn't move either. It stared at me.

It seemed like an hour, but it was probably only a minute or two that we stood there and stared at each other. Then the bear began to move.

It went back into the trees, went around me, and continued its climb uphill. It had probably been down to the lake for a drink of water.

I too continued on my way after I was sure the bear was gone.

"It was strange," I thought, "I wasn't planning to harm the bear, and the bear wasn't intending to harm me. Yet we were both afraid of each other."

Guess the meanings of words.

*Read each section of the story. Then read the statements that follow each section. Put **T** in front of each statement that is true. Put **F** in front of each statement that is false.*

One day I was hiking in the Mission Mountains of Montana and came to a large lake which was surrounded by big rocks and tall pine trees. The lake was formed by a stream which ran down from the mountains.

_____   1.   There were rocks and pine trees all around the lake.

_____   2.   Water ran down from the mountains into the lake.

_____   3.   *Surround* and *form* have the same meaning here.

_____   4.   *Form* means "make."

"Don't move," I told myself. I stood there and stared at the bear. I never moved my eyes. My heart began to beat faster and faster.

The bear didn't move either. It stared at me.

_____   5.   When you stare at something, you look at it.

_____   6.   You move your eyes when you stare at something.

"It was strange," I thought, "I wasn't planning to harm the bear, and the bear wasn't intending to harm me. Yet we were both afraid of each other."

_____   7.   The writer was not intending to harm the bear.

_____   8.   The bear was intending to harm the writer.

_____   9.   *Planning* and *intending* have similar meanings here.

Use words in context.

Write one word in each blank.

formed   surrounded   upstream   waterfall

The lake was _____ by a stream and was

_____ by rocks and trees. _____ was a

beautiful _____.

intended   stared

The author and the bear just _____ at each other.

Neither _____ to harm the other.

Check your comprehension.

Read each section of the story. Then answer the questions by circling the letter in front of the correct answer.

One day I was hiking in the Mission Mountains of Montana and came to a large lake which was surrounded by big rocks and tall pine trees. The lake was formed by a stream which ran down from the mountains.

1. What was all around the lake?
   a. mountains
   b. rocks and trees

2. Where did the water in the lake come from?
   a. from the mountains
   b. from the rocks and pine trees

Someone told me that I could see a beautiful waterfall if I climbed upstream for about 30 minutes, and so I did.

The waterfall was indeed very beautiful. Water fell into a clear pool of cool water from a rock about 100 feet above.

3. Where did the author go to see the waterfall?
   a. up the mountain
   b. down the mountain

4. Did the author like the waterfall?
   a. yes
   b. no

I sat on a rock near the pool and ate some sandwiches I had brought with me. Some mountain climbers walked by; each of them greeted me with a "hello" or a "hi."

5. Were the mountain climbers friendly?

    a. yes
    b. no

After I finished my lunch, I began to walk slowly back down the trail to the lake. Suddenly, I heard a noise and looked up. Fifty feet in front of me was a big, black bear. It had just come out of the trees and was standing in the trail.

6. Who was higher up the mountain?

    a. the bear
    b. the writer

7. How close were the author and the bear to each other?

    a. They were rather close together.
    b. They were very far apart.

"Don't move," I told myself. I stood there and stared at the bear. I never moved my eyes. My heart began to beat faster and faster.
    The bear didn't move either. It stared at me.

8. Did the author and the bear look at each other?

    a. yes
    b. no

It seemed like an hour, but it was probably only a minute or two that we stood there and stared at each other. Then the bear began to move.

9. About how long did the author and the bear stand and stare at each other?

    a. about an hour
    b. one or two minutes

It went back into the trees, went around me, and continued its climb uphill. It had probably been down to the lake for a drink of water.
    I too continued on my way after I was sure the bear was gone.

10. Which way did the bear go after it saw the author?

    a. down the mountain
    b. up the mountain

11. Did the bear walk right past the author?
    a. yes
    b. no

    "It was strange," I thought, "I wasn't planning to harm the bear, and the bear wasn't intending to harm me. Yet we were both afraid of each other."

12. What did the author think was strange?
    a. The author thought it was strange that the bear did not intend any harm.
    b. The author thought it was strange that they were both afraid even though neither intended to harm the other.

Use information to make guesses.

Read each section of the story. Then answer the questions by writing the number of the appropriate sentence in the parentheses.

   (1) The waterfall was indeed very beautiful. (2) Water fell into a clear pool of cool water from a rock about 100 feet above.

 1. Which sentence tells you that the author liked the waterfall? (   )

   (1) "Don't move," I told myself. (2) I stood there and stared at the bear. (3) I never moved my eyes. (4) My heart beat faster and faster.

 2. Which sentence tells you that the author knew what to do when meeting a bear? (   )
 3. Which sentence tells you that the author was afraid? (   )

Recall the story.

Tell or write the main parts of the story. Do not look back at the story. Use the following phrases as a guide. Be sure to place events in the correct order.

> circled around
> met a bear on the way down
> stared at each other
> to see a waterfall
> was hiking

Talk about your experience.

Have you ever met a wild animal while hiking somewhere? Share your experience with your classmates.

Part Three — BEAR ATTACKS

Listening

Listen for the main idea.

Your teacher will give you some information. Listen to the information. Then choose the sentence which best tells what the information is about.

a. Our chances of being attacked by a bear when we visit national parks are very small.

b. Bears will not attack if we are careful about where we keep food and where we put garbage.

c. If we come across a bear while hiking, it will probably run away.

Listen for words.

Fill in the blanks while listening to the information again. Use the following words and expressions:

accidentally	in danger of
attacked	run away
campers	statistics
garbage	trouble
hikers	

Are people who visit national parks _____ being

_____ by a bear? We have seen from _____

that the chances of being _____ by a bear are very small.

We have also seen that if you _____ meet a bear while

hiking, the bear will probably _____. If _____

and _____ are careful about where they keep their food

and about where they throw their _____, they will probably

never have any _____ with bears.

Match words with definitions.

Read the information. Then choose words to match the definitions.

Statistics show that campers can avoid being injured by bears if they do not try to get close to them, and if they are careful about where they keep their food and about where they throw their garbage.

Which word in the preceding paragraph means

a. food that we throw away?   _____

b. to keep away from?   _____

c. numbers?   _____

Use words in context.

Write one word in each blank.

avoid   garbage   statistics

According to _____, one way to _____
_____ bears is to put your _____ in a proper place.

Check your comprehension.

Your teacher will ask you some questions about the information. Listen to the questions. Then write out the answers to the questions.

1. _____.
2. _____.
3. We should _____
   and _____.

Listen to the information again. Check your answers while you listen.

Reading

Read for the main ideas.

Read the information quickly. Then answer the questions by circling the letter in front of the correct answer.

1. What is the main idea of the reading?
   a. Many people visit national parks every year.
   b. On rare occasions, bears attack people.
   c. People can visit parks with little risk of being attacked by a bear.

2. In general, what do the statistics in paragraphs three and four show?
   a. They show that the parks are safe.
   b. They show that the parks are dangerous.

Bear Attacks in National Parks

The national parks in the United States attract millions of visitors every year. People come to see the natural beauty preserved in these parks and to see wildlife.

Grizzly bears run wild in some of the U.S. national parks. On rare occasions, one of these bears attacks and injures or kills someone. One such attack occurred in 1967 in Glacier National Park. Grizzly bears there attacked and killed two women.

These rare attacks are primarily on people in campgrounds and on hikers in the back country. The attacks are publicized widely in newspapers and on television news, and people become afraid and ask if grizzly bears should be banned from the parks.

Statistics show, however, that people who visit parks are not in great danger of attack from grizzly bears. During the first 97 years following the establishment of national parks, grizzlies killed only five people and injured 25 others.

Even as more and more people visit the parks, the number of bear attacks hasn't increased enough to cause great concern. The attack rate in 1960 was one attack every three years. Despite the increase of visitors to the parks since then, the rate has risen to only about five attacks per year. This rate is still very low. In fact, it amounts to only about one attack for every one million visitors to national parks.

While visitors should, of course, exercise caution when they are near bears, it appears from the statistics that they can enjoy the scenery and recreation of the national parks with very little risk of being attacked by grizzly bears.

Guess the meanings of words.

Read the information. Then circle the letter in front of the answer that best defines the word.

The national parks in the United States attract millions of visitors every year. People come to see the natural beauty preserved in these parks and to see wildlife.

1. Attract
   a. Millions of people like the parks and visit them.
   b. Millions of people think about visiting the parks.

2. Preserve
   a. The parks have lost their natural beauty.
   b. The parks still have their natural beauty.

3. Wildlife

    a. Animals that live in the mountains and forests are wildlife.

    b. Animals that live on farms and ranches are wildlife.

These rare attacks are primarily on people in campgrounds and on hikers in the back country. The attacks are publicized widely in newspapers and on television news, and people become afraid and ask if grizzly bears should be banned from the parks.

4. Primarily

    a. Few bear attacks are on people in campgrounds and on hikers in the back country.

    b. Most bear attacks are on people in campgrounds and on hikers in the back country.

5. Publicize

    a. *To publicize* means "to let other people know about something."

    b. When you publicize something, you do not tell other people about it.

6. Ban

    a. *Ban* means "to let in."

    b. *Ban* means "to keep out."

During the first 97 years following the establishment of national parks, grizzlies killed only five people and injured 25 others.

7. Establish

    a. *To establish* means "to end."

    b. *To establish* means "to begin."

Even as more and more people visit the parks, the number of bear attacks hasn't increased enough to cause great concern.

8. Concern

    a. If we are concerned about something, we are worried about it.

    b. We are not worried about something, when we are concerned about it.

While visitors should, of course, exercise caution when they are near bears, it appears from the statistics that they can enjoy the scenery and recreation of the national parks with very little risk of being attacked by grizzly bears.

9. Exercise caution

    a. You are not careful when you exercise caution.

    b. You are careful when you exercise caution.

10. Risk

   a. When there is little risk, there is a lot of danger.
   b. When there is little risk, there is little danger.

Use words in context.

Write one word in each blank.

attract   caution   risk

Food and garbage _____ bears, so if you exercise _____ there is little _____ of a bear attacking you.

banned   establishing   preserve   wildlife

The government _____ private business from _____ tourist attractions in national parks in order to _____ _____.

concerned   primarily   publicize

Bear attacks are _____ on people in campgrounds and hikers in the back country. Newspapers become _____ about these attacks and _____ them.

Check your comprehension.

Write out answers to the following questions.

1. Are there grizzly bears in national parks?

2. What happened in the 1967 bear attack in Glacier National Park?

3. What happens when people hear of such attacks?

4. The reading gives statistics that show that people who visit national parks are not in great danger of being attacked by bears. List those statistics.

   a. _____
   b. _____
   c. _____

5. What conclusion is made in the reading?

Summarize the reading.

Fill in the blanks to make a sentence that summarizes the reading.

attacked   danger   statistics   visit

_____ show that people who _____
national parks are not in much _____ of being
_____ by bears.

Tell how you would feel.

Would you be afraid that a bear might attack you if you visited a national park?
Why, or why not?

Part Four

Outside Reading

Find more information about bears.

*Find a book in the library about bears, or look for information about
bears in an encyclopedia. Try to find pictures of different kinds of bears.*

Lesson 8

Part One — **THE ELDERLY**

Listening

Listen for the main idea.

Your teacher will give you some information. Listen to the information. Then choose the answer which best tells what the information is about.

a. United States
b. Social Security
c. the elderly

Listen for words.

Fill in the blanks while listening to the information again. Use the following words or expressions:

> elderly   retire
> government   Social Security
> officially

_____ means old. _____ people,

therefore, are old people. In the United States, people are

_____ _____ when they reach the age of
65. That is when most people _____ from their jobs and
begin receiving _____. _____ is money
_____ people receive every month from the

_____.

Guess the meanings of words.

Read the information. Then read the statements following the informa-
*tion. Put **T** in front of statements that are true. Put **F** in front of state-*
ments that are false.

The United States Bureau of the Census, the government office that
counts all Americans every 10 years, considers a person to be old, or elderly,
from age 65. In other words, people are officially elderly when they reach 65
years of age.

_____   1.   The United States Bureau of the Census counts people.
_____   2.   An *old person* is different from an *elderly person*.
_____   3.   *Official* decisions are made by the government.

People stop working when they retire. Therefore, they no longer receive
money from their employer. Instead, they get money from the government.
This money is one of the Social Security benefits that people receive.

_____   4.   Retired people receive Social Security benefits.
_____   5.   Social Security is money people receive from an employer.
_____   6.   People who are working are retired.

Use words in context.

Write one word or expression in each blank.

Census   elderly   officially   retires   Social Security

According to the Bureau of the _____, a person is
_____ _____ when he or she is 65 years
old. At that time, a person _____ and begins to receive
_____ benefits.

Check your comprehension.

Your teacher will ask you some questions about the information. Listen to the questions. Then write out the answers to the questions.

1. _____.
2. _____.
3. _____ and _____
   _____.

Listen to the information again. Check your answers while you listen.

Reading

Preview the reading.

The following three charts are about the elderly in the United States. List what each chart is about.

Chart 1: _____
Chart 2: _____
Chart 3: _____

CHART 1   PERCENTAGE OF PEOPLE 65 YEARS OF AGE OR OLDER

YEAR	PERCENTAGE	YEAR	PERCENTAGE
1920	4.6	1990	12.7
1930	5.4	2000	13.1
1940	6.8	2010	13.9
1950	8.1	2020	17.3
1960	9.3	2030	21.1
1970	9.9	2040	21.6
1980	11.3	2050	21.9

CHART 2   PERCENTAGE OF ELDERLY IN AGE GROUPS ABOVE 65

YEAR	1950	1960	1970	1980	1990	2000	2010	2020
AGE GROUP								
65 to 69	40.7	37.7	35.5	34.2	31.5	26 0	29.8	32.3
70 to 74	27.8	28.6	27.2	26.6	25.3	24.5	21.9	25.6
75 to 79	17.4	18.5	19.2	18.7	19.6	20.7	17.1	17.0
80 to 84	9.3	9.6	11.5	11.6	12.8	14.2	13.9	10.8
85 & over	4.8	5.6	7.1	8.8	10.9	14.7	17.4	14.3

CHART 3   MALES PER 100 FEMALES AT VARIOUS AGE GROUPS

YEAR	1950	1960	1970	1980	1990	2000	2010	2020
AGE GROUP								
Under 15	103.3	103.4	103.9	104.6	104.8	104.9	104.0	104.9
15 to 29	98.7	97.7	97 8	101.9	103.1	103.5	103.7	103.7
30 to 44	97.4	95.5	95.2	96.9	98.8	100.2	100.9	101.2
45 to 59	99.8	96.9	93.4	92.0	93.3	94.9	96.6	97.6
60 to 64	100.4	91.2	87.7	86.2	86.3	87.9	90.0	92.0
65 to 69	94.0	87.8	80.7	80.0	80.4	82.1	84.3	86.4
70 to 74	91.3	85.3	73.9	72.4	73.2	74.2	76.1	78.7
75 to 84	85.0	77.4	65.9	58.9	59.3	60.0	61.1	64.0
85 & over	70.0	63.8	53.2	43.7	38.6	37.2	36.3	36.0

Source: 1980 census figures.

Find specific information.

1. Refer to Chart 1. Give the percentage of Americans who were/will be 65 years of age or older in each of the following years.

   a. 1920: _____

   b. 1980: _____

   c. 2050: _____

2. Is the percentage of elderly people increasing or decreasing?

3. Refer to Chart 2. Read the statements. Put **T** in front of each statement that is true. Put **F** in front of each statement that is false.

_____ a.   In 1950, 40.7 percent of the elderly were in the 65 to 69 age group.

_____ b.   In 2020, 14.3 percent of the elderly will be 85 years or older.

_____ c.   From the data (information) in the chart, we can guess that the lives of Americans are becoming shorter.

_____ d.   There will be more people over 85 years of age in 2010 than there were in 1950.

4. Refer to Chart 3. Read the statements. Put **T** in front of each statement that is true. Put **F** in front of each statement that is false.

_____ a.   In 1980, there were 86.2 males for every 100 females in the 60 to 64 age group.

_____ b.   In 2000, there will be 104.9 females in the under 15 age group for every 100 males.

_____ c.   In 2020, about two-thirds of the elderly in the 85 and over group will be women.

_____ d.   This chart shows that women live longer than men.

Summarize the information.

Complete the sentences. Use the following words.

increasing   longer (2)   males

1. Chart 1 shows that the percentage of elderly is _____.
2. Chart 2 shows that Americans are living _____.
3. Chart 3 shows that females live _____ than _____
_____.

Part Two — THE OLD MAN AND THE BOY

Listening

Listen for the Main Idea.

Your teacher will give you some information. Listen to the information. Then choose the answer which best tells what the information is about.

a. an elderly man and his grandson

b. mountain sunsets

c. camping in the mountains

Listen for words.

Fill in the blanks while listening to the information again. Use the following words or expressions:

campground	little boy
camping	old man
grandfather	sunset
grandson	

An _____ and his three-year-old _____

_____ were _____ in the mountains. In the evening,

the _____ left the _____ and climbed up

to a high place to see the sun go down. The _____ _____

followed the _ _____ _____, but he did not want to see the

_____. He just wanted his _____ to go

back to the tent.

Guess the meanings of words.

*Read the information. Then read the statements following the information. Put **T** in front of statements that are true. Put **F** in front of statements that are false.*

The old man was first, climbing to a high place to see the sun go down. He liked to see sunsets. Following behind him was his three-year-old grandson.

_____ 1. The boy was following the old man.

_____ 2. The old man was walking in front of the boy.

_____ 3. The old man did not like to watch the sun go down.

_____ 4. A *sunset* is when the sun goes down.

Use words in context.

Write one word in each blank.

followed   grandson   sunset

When the old man climbed up to a high place to see the _____,

his _____ _____ him.

Check your comprehension.

Your teacher will ask you some questions about the information. Listen to the questions. Then write out the answers to the questions.

1. _____.
2. _____.
3. _____.

Listen to the information again. Check your answers while you listen.

Reading

Read for the main ideas.

Read the story quickly. Then write answers to the following questions.

1. Why did the old man climb up to the ridge?

2. Who followed him?

3. Did the old man enjoy what he saw?

4. What did the boy want the old man to do?

The Old Man and the Boy

The old man had left the campsite and was climbing slowly to the ridge that overlooked a meadow and the mountains beyond.

Following some distance behind him was a little three-year-old boy, whose short legs had trouble climbing up and over the rocks that lay in the trail.

The old man reached the ridge and sat down on a large rock just as the sun was about to set.

Pine trees, tall and straight, stood on the mountain slope. Below in the green, grassy meadow, the water in a meandering stream reflected setting sunlight.

The little boy caught up with the old man and sat down next to him.

"Grandpa, why did you come way up here?" the little boy asked.

"I want to watch the setting sun. And maybe I can see some deer."

"Grandpa," the little boy replied, "you can't see the sun. It's gonna* go behind that mountain. And it's gonna get dark. Come back to the tent!"

*Gonna is a spoken form of *going to*.

"Wait. Maybe we can see some deer when it gets a little darker."

"There're no deer here! I just see some dead trees and old, broken rocks. We have to go back to the tent, Grandpa."

"But look at the river. See the sun shining on it?"

"That's not a river. It's a big snake. Let's get out of here. It's gonna get us."

"Maybe to you it looks like a snake from up here. But to me it's a beautiful river."

"That's not a pretty river, Grandpa. And those are not pretty rocks and trees. Let's get out of here!"

"No, wait. I want to stay here a little longer. I like these trees, these rocks, that river, and those mountains."

"Grandpa, you can't like it here. Look, there's no cars and trucks down there. And we don't have a TV. I'm gonna get my toy bulldozer and dump truck. I'm gonna pick up these rocks and those dead trees and throw them away."

The sun had just set. The old man raised himself up from the rock. "OK, let's go back to the tent."

He took the little boy by the hand; they slowly walked back down toward the campground.

"Someday, you're going to like all this," the old man foretold.

The little boy said nothing. He was happy just to be going back to the tent with his grandpa.

Match words with definitions.

Read each section of the story. Then read the definitions or synonymous phrases (phrases that have the same meaning) listed after each section. Find the words in each section that match the definitions or phrases.

The old man had left the campsite and was climbing slowly to the ridge that overlooked a meadow and the mountains beyond.

1. A place in a campground where you put up a tent: _____
2. The long, narrow top of a mountain or a slope: _____
3. To look down at something from a high place: _____
4. Farther away than the meadow: _____

The old man reached the ridge and sat down on a large rock just as the sun was about to set.

Pine trees, tall and straight, stood on the mountain slope. Below in the green, grassy meadow, the water in a meandering stream reflected setting sunlight.

5. The sun was about to go down: _____
6. An open area with grass: _____

7. A river: _____

8. A river that turns a lot: _____

9. Sunlight that is shining back from the river: _____

"Grandpa," the little boy replied, "you can't see the sun. It's gonna go behind that mountain. And it's gonna get dark. Come back to the tent!"

10. Going to go: _____

11. Going to get dark: _____

"That's not a pretty river, Grandpa. And those are not pretty rocks and trees. Let's get out of here!"

12. Let's go away from this place: _____

"Someday, you're going to like all this," the old man foretold.

13. To say what will happen in the future: _____

Use words in context.

Write one word or expression in each blank.

beyond	meandering stream	ridge
campsite	overlooked	setting
meadow	reflected	

The _____ was near the top of a _____ _____ that _____ a _____. In this meadow was a _____ that _____ the _____ sunlight. _____ the meadow were some mountains.

foretold	get out of here

The little boy said, "Let's _____." But the old man _____, "Someday, you are going to like all this."

Determine the meanings of pronouns.

Write a noun in each blank. The noun must have the same meaning as the word just before the parentheses.

The old man had left the campsite and was climbing slowly to the ridge that overlooked a meadow and the mountains beyond.

Following some distance behind him (_____) was a little three-year-old boy, whose (_____) short legs had trouble climbing up and over the rocks that lay in the trail.

. . . The little boy caught up with the old man and sat down next to him (_____).

"Grandpa, why did you come way up here (_____)?" the little boy asked.

"I want to watch the setting sun. And maybe I can see some deer."

"Grandpa," the little boy replied, "you can't see the sun. It's (_____) gonna go behind that mountain. . . ."

. . . "But look at the river. See the sun shining on it (_____)?"

"That's not a river. It's (_____) a big snake. Let's get out of here! It's (_____) gonna get us."

"Maybe to you it (_____) looks like a snake from up here. But to me (_____) it's a beautiful river."

Check your comprehension.

*Read each section of the story. Then read the statements that follow each section. Put **T** in front of each statement that is true. Put **F** in front of each statement that is false.*

The old man had left the campsite and was climbing slowly to the ridge that overlooked a meadow and the mountains beyond.

_____ 1. The old man was climbing to a place higher than the campsite.

_____ 2. There was a meadow on the other side of the ridge.

_____ 3. Mountains were between the ridge and the meadow.

Following some distance behind him was a little three-year-old boy, whose short legs had trouble climbing up and over the rocks that lay in the trail.

_____ 4. The little boy was walking beside his grandfather.

_____ 5. The little boy could walk up the trail easily.

The old man reached the ridge and sat down on a large rock just as the sun was about to set.

_____ 6. After the old man climbed to the top of the ridge, he sat down on a rock.

_____ 7. The sun was still high in the sky.

Pine trees, tall and straight, stood on the mountain slope. Below in the green, grassy meadow, the water in a meandering stream reflected setting sunlight.

_____ 8. There were pine trees on the mountain.

_____ 9. There was a river in the meadow.

The little boy caught up with the old man and sat down next to him.

_____ 10. The little boy walked up to the place where his grandfather was and sat down beside him.

"Grandpa, why did you come way up here?" the little boy asked.
"I want to watch the setting sun. And maybe I can see some deer."

_____ 11. The old man climbed the ridge to watch the sun go down.

_____ 12. The old man is certain he will see some deer.

"Grandpa," the little boy replied, "you can't see the sun. It's gonna go behind that mountain. And it's gonna get dark. Come back to the tent!"

_____ 13. The old man will not be able to see the sun set.

_____ 14. It is going to get dark.

"Wait. Maybe we can see some deer when it gets a little darker."
"There're no deer here! I just see some dead trees and old, broken rocks. We have to go back to the tent, Grandpa."
"But look at the river. See the sun shining on it?"
"That's not a river. It's a big snake. Let's get out of here! It's gonna get us."
"Maybe to you it looks like a snake from up here. But to me it's a beautiful river."

_____ 15. There were no deer near that place.

_____ 16. There was no river.

_____ 17. There was no snake.

"That's not a pretty river, Grandpa. And those are not pretty rocks and trees. Let's get out of here!"
"No, wait. I want to stay here a little longer. I like these trees, these rocks, that river, and those mountains."

"Grandpa, you can't like it here. Look, there's no cars and trucks down there. And we don't have a TV. I'm gonna get my toy bulldozer and dump truck. I'm gonna pick up these rocks and those dead trees and throw them away."

_____ 18. The old man wanted to stay there longer.

_____ 19. The boy wanted to stay there longer.

_____ 20. The old man is interested in nature.

_____ 21. The boy is not interested in nature.

_____ 22. The boy is not interested in cars, trucks, and televisions.

The sun had just set. The old man raised himself up from the rock. "OK, let's go back to the tent."

He took the little boy by the hand; they slowly walked back down toward the campground.

"Someday, you're going to like all this," the old man foretold.

The little boy said nothing. He was happy just to be going back to the tent with his grandpa.

_____ 23. The old man thinks that the little boy will like nature when he gets older.

_____ 24. The little boy wanted to be back at the tent with his grandfather.

Guess the meanings from context.

*Read each section of the story. Then read the statements. Put **T** in front of each statement that you think is true. Put **F** in front of each statement that you think is false.*

Pine trees, tall and straight, stood on the mountain slope. Below in the green, grassy meadow, the water in a meandering stream reflected setting sunlight.

_____ 1. The view from the ridge was beautiful.

The little boy caught up with the old man and sat down next to him. "Grandpa, why did you come way up here?" the little boy asked.

"I want to watch the setting sun. And maybe I can see some deer."

"Grandpa," the little boy replied, "you can't see the sun. It's gonna go behind that mountain. And it's gonna get dark. Come back to the tent!"

_____ 2. The little boy climbed the ridge to see the view.

_____ 3. The little boy climbed the ridge because he wanted to be with his grandfather.

"Grandpa, you can't like it here. Look, there's no cars and trucks down there. And we don't have a TV. I'm gonna get my toy bulldozer and dump truck. I'm gonna pick up these rocks and those dead trees and throw them away."

_____   4. The little boy is too young to understand his grandfather's feelings about nature.

The sun had just set. The old man raised himself up from the rock. "OK, let's go back to the tent."

He took the little boy by the hand; they slowly walked back down toward the campground.

_____   5. The sun was still shining as they walked back to the camp-ground.

"Someday, you're going to like all this," the old man foretold.

The little boy said nothing. He was happy just to be going back to the tent with his grandpa.

_____   6. The little boy understood what his grandfather said to him.
_____   7. The little boy loves his grandfather very much.
_____   8. The old man knows the boy will change his thinking over the years.

Summarize the story.

Fill in the blanks. You may look back at the reading.

An old man climbed _____. His grandson followed _____. The old man wanted _____. The view from the ridge was beautiful, but the boy wanted his grandfather _____. The little boy didn't _____.

Part Three — LIFE EXPECTANCY

Listening

Listen for the main idea.

Your teacher will give you some information. Listen to the information. Then choose the answer which best tells what the information is about.

a. There will be more elderly people over the years.

b. The Bureau of the Census has issued a report about the elderly.

c. The number of elderly is increasing; Americans need to think about how to take care of them.

Listen for words.

Fill in the blanks while listening to the information again. Use the following words, numbers, and expressions:

Census   increasing
coming years   projects
elderly   22
                2050

Americans are living longer Therefore, the number of elderly is _____ year by year. The U.S Bureau of the

__ _____ ___ _____ that by the year

_____ almost _____ percent of all

Americans will be _____. Who will take care of so many

_____? How will the economic and health needs of the

_____ be met? These and other questions are ones that

Americans must answer over the _____.

Guess the meanings of words.

*Read the information. Then read the statements following the information. Put **T** in front of each statement that is true. Put **F** in front of each statement that is false.*

The Bureau of the Census counts all the people who live in the United States every 10 years. These statistics show many things about the people in the United States, including how many Americans there are and how old they are. These statistics also help the Bureau to project for coming years the number of people and their ages.

_____ 1. Statistics are people.

_____ 2. Statistics are numbers.

_____ 3. In the preceding paragraph, *project for the coming years* means "to predict or tell about the future."

_____ 4. *Over the coming years* means "right now."

_____ 5. *Over the coming years* refers to a time in the past.

Use words in context.

Write one word or expression in each blank.

census   coming years   projects   statistics

Using _____ from the last _____, the
government _____ that the number of elderly will increase
over the _____.

Check your comprehension.

*Your teacher will ask you some questions about the information. Listen
to the questions. Then write out the answers to the questions.*

1. _____.
2. _____.
3. _____.

Listen to the information again. Check your answers while you listen.

Reading

Read for the main ideas.

*Read the information quickly. Then write answers to the following
questions.*

1. What is happening to the life expectancy of Americans?

2. What is happening to the number of elderly people?

3. Who live longer, men or women?

Life Expectancy

The life expectancy of Americans is increasing. According to
statistics put out by the U.S. Bureau of the Census, the life expectancy
for men has increased from 47 years in 1900 to 69.8 years in 1980.
For women, it has gone up from 49 years to 77.7 years. By 2050, the
life expectancy is projected to be 75 years for men and 83.6 years for
women. Improved public health, better sanitation, and control of
diseases are the primary reasons why Americans are living longer.

Because life expectancy is increasing, the number of elderly people* is growing rapidly. The Census Bureau predicts that 65 million people will be 65 years of age or older by the year 2030. This contrasts with only 26 million people who were 65 or older in 1980.

Women, whose life expectancy is higher than that of men, make up the majority of the elderly. In 1980, for example, there were only 68 men for every 100 women 65 years of age or over and only 55 men for every 100 women 75 years of age or older.

Guess the meanings of words.

Read the information quickly. Then read the statements that follow. Put **T** *in front of each statement that is true. Put* **F** *in front of each statement that is false.*

The life expectancy of Americans is increasing. According to statistics put out by the U.S. Bureau of the Census, the life expectancy for men has increased from 47 years in 1900 to 69.8 years in 1980. For women, it has gone up from 49 years to 77.7 years. By 2050, the life expectancy is projected to be 75 years for men and 83.6 years for women. Improved public health, better sanitation, and control of diseases are the primary reasons why Americans are living longer.

_____ 1. *Life expectancy* refers to how many years a person might live.

_____ 2. *Life expectancy* refers to the exact number of years a person will live.

_____ 3. *Improve* means "to make something worse."

_____ 4. *Primary reasons* are important reasons.

_____ 5. *Diseases* are illnesses.

_____ 6. People can die earlier because of diseases.

Because life expectancy is increasing, the number of elderly people is growing rapidly. The Census Bureau projects that 65 million people will be 65 years of age or older by the year 2030. This contrasts with only 26 million people who were 65 or older in 1980.

_____ 7. *Rapidly* means "quickly."

_____ 8. Things that *contrast* are the same.

Elderly is defined by the U.S. Bureau of the Census as referring to people who are 65 years of age or older. This is the age at which most people retire and begin receiving Social Security benefits from the government.

Women, whose life expectancy is higher than that of men, make up the majority of the elderly. In 1980, for example, there were only 68 men for every 100 women 65 years of age or over and only 55 men for every 100 women 75 years of age or older.

_____ 9. *Majority* means "the fewest."

_____ 10. *Death rate* refers to the percentage of people who die at a certain age.

Use words in context.

Write one word or expression in each blank.

diseases   improved   life expectancy   primary

The _____ of people is increasing. A _____ _____ reason for this is _____ control of _____.

elderly   rapidly

The number of _____ is increasing _____ _____.

contrast   life expectancy   majority

The _____ of the elderly are women, who have a higher _____ than men. The life expectancy for women in 1980 was 77.7 years. In _____, the life expectancy for men was only 68.8 years.

Outline the reading.

Fill in the blanks. You may look back at the reading.

I. **Life expectancy**

Men	Year	Women
_____	_____	_____
_____	_____	_____
_____	_____	_____

II. **Reasons for longer life expectancy**

_____

_____

_____

III. **Number of elderly, 65 years or older**

Year   **Number**

_____   _____

_____   _____

Check your comprehension.

Answer the following questions.

1. Does the reading say that the life expectancy of Americans is getting longer or shorter?

2. Why are there more elderly women than elderly men?

3. According to the Bureau of the Census, who is an elderly person?

Summarize the reading.

Fill in the blanks. Use the following expressions:

> a longer life expectancy   increasing
> elderly is increasing   the majority

The life expectancy of Americans is _____. As a result, the number of _____.
Of the elderly, women make up _____
because they have _____.

Use information to make guesses.

Guess the answer to the following question.

Do you think Americans will be able to take care of the elderly in the year 2050? Why, or why not?

Part Four

Outside Reading

Find out more about the problems of the elderly.

What are some of the problems of the elderly today? Look up elderly *in an encyclopedia. What does the encyclopedia say about the problems of the elderly?*

Lesson 9

Part One — **TROPICAL CYCLONES**

Listening

Listen for the main Idea.

Your teacher will give you some information. Listen to the information. Then choose the answer which best tells what the information is about.

a. oceans

b. storms

c. tropical cyclones

Listen for words.

Fill in the blanks while listening to the information again. Use the following words or expressions:

cyclones	storms
develop	tropical
hurricanes	typhoons
severe	

Tropical _____ are very large storms. They _____ over the oceans in _____ areas. They are called by different names, depending on which part of the world they _____ in. They are called _____ in the Atlantic Ocean, _____ in the Pacific Ocean, and _____ in the Indian Ocean. Over the years, there have been many very _____ tropical storms. Some of these _____ have killed several hundred thousand people.

Guess the meanings of words.

*Read the information. Then read the statements following the information. Put **T** in front of each statement that is true. Put **F** in front of each statement that is false.*

There are different kinds of storms. Some storms, such as rainstorms and snowstorms, are not usually severe and do not cause damage. Other storms, such as tropical cyclones and tornadoes, are severe and cause much damage.

_____ 1. Four different kinds of storms are mentioned in the paragraph.

_____ 2. Rainstorms and snowstorms are severe storms.

_____ 3. Tropical cyclones and tornadoes are severe storms.

_____ 4. A severe storm causes much damage.

Use words in context.

Write one word in each blank.

cyclone	severe

A _____ tropical _____ killed 300,000 people in India in 1737.

Check your comprehension.

Your teacher will ask you some questions about the information. Listen to the questions. Then write out the answers to the questions.

1. _____.
2. _____.
3. _____.
4. _____.

Listen to the information again. Check your answers while you listen.

Reading

Preview the reading.

Look at the chart quickly. Then answer the following questions.

1. What is the chart about?

2. What kinds of information does the chart give about each storm?

a. _____

b. _____

c. _____

KILLER TROPICAL CYCLONES
(Storms with more than 1,000 deaths)

YEAR	COUNTRY	ESTIMATED DEATHS
1737	India	300,000
1789	India	20,000
1864	India	80,000
1876	India	200,000
1881	Vietnam	300,000
1882	India	100,000
1900	United States	6,000
1930	Dominican Republic	8,000
1932	Cuba	4,000
1934	Japan	3,066
1942	India	40,000
1945	Japan	3,122
1959	Japan	5,378
1960	Bangladesh	6,000
1960	Bangladesh	4,000
1963	Haiti & Cuba	3,500
1963	Bangladesh	12,000
1965	Bangladesh	45,000
1970	Bangladesh	200,000
1971	India	10,000
1974	Honduras	5,000
1977	India	3,000
1979	West Indies	2,000
1984	Philippines	1,360
1985	Bangladesh	10,000

Find specific information.

Write out answers to the questions.

1. Look at the chart headings.
   a. Does the chart list every hurricane that killed people?
   b. Does the chart list the exact number of deaths?

2. Look at the arrangement of the storms listed on the chart. Are the storms arranged according to year or according to the number of people who died?

3. Which storms listed on the chart killed the most people? Which storm killed the fewest people?

Use information to solve problems.

For each country, write the total number of fatalities (number of people killed) in the storms listed on the chart.

Bangladesh   _____

Cuba/Haiti   _____ 7,500 _____

Dominican Republic _____

Honduras   _____

India   _____

Japan   _____

Philippines   _____

United States   _____

Vietnam   _____

West Indies   _____

Which country has had the most fatalities?

Which country has had the fewest fatalities?

Summarize the listening and chart.

Fill in the blanks. Use the following words and numbers.

> develop   killed   tropical   1970   200,000

_____ cyclones are large storms that _____ over the ocean in tropical areas. Thousands of people have been _____ by these storms. In Bangladesh, for example, _____ people were killed in a storm in _____ .

Part Two — THE TORNADO

Listening

Listen for the main idea.

Your teacher will give you some information. Listen to the information. Then choose the sentence which best tells what the information is about.

a. It tells about a tornado.

b. It tells how to take shelter in basements during tornadoes.

c. It is about tornadoes that occur in the middle part of the United States.

Listen for words.

Fill in the blanks while listening to the information again. Use the following words or expressions.

basement	storms	twisting
funnel-shaped	take shelter	windstorms
hang down	tornadoes	

_____ are very severe _____

_____. They occur often in the middle part of the United

States during the spring and summer. These _____ can

destroy almost everything that they hit. Tornadoes look like dark

_____ clouds that _____ from the sky.

They make a loud noise. When a tornado comes, people usually

_____ in the _____ of their homes.

Guess the meanings of words.

*Read the information. Then read the statements that follow the information. Put **T** in front of statements that are true. Put **F** in front of statements that are false.*

A tornado has twisting, or spinning, winds that turn around and around at more than 300 miles per hour. A tornado looks like a funnel-shaped cloud that hangs down toward the earth from the sky. The cloud is wide at the top and narrow at the bottom.

_____ 1. The winds of a tornado spin slowly.

_____ 2. Twisting winds turn around and around.

_____ 3. Spinning winds turn around and around.

_____ 4. A tornado cloud does not look like a funnel.

_____ 5. A cloud that "hangs down toward the earth" has its top in the sky and its bottom near or at the earth.

_____ 6. The wide part of a tornado cloud is near or at the earth.

To protect themselves when a tornado comes, many people take shelter by going down to the basement in their houses.

_____ 7. People protect themselves by going to the basement.

_____ 8. People take shelter by going to the basement.

_____ 9. *Take shelter* means "to go somewhere to protect yourself."

Use words in context.

Write one word in each blank.

basement   funnel-shaped   hanging   shelter   twisting

After she looked out the window and saw a _____,
_____ cloud _____ down from the sky,
she took _____ in the _____.

Check your comprehension.

Your teacher will ask you some questions about the information. Listen to the questions. Then write out the answers to the questions.

1. _____.
2. _____.
3. _____.
4. _____.
5. _____.

Listen to the information again. Check your answers while you listen.

Reading

Read for the main ideas.

Read the story quickly. Find the answers to the following questions.

1. What kind of day was it when the tornado came?

2. Where did the mother and children go for shelter?

3. Was anyone killed?

4. Was anyone injured?

The Tornado

The summer day was very hot. I was just a child then and was playing outside with my friends.

In the late afternoon, dark clouds began to gather in the western sky, and later the wind began to blow. The clouds moved faster and faster toward us.

All of a sudden, the sky turned yellow. I could hear my mother shouting to us to get into the house immediately. While running toward the house, I saw a dark, gray funnel-shaped cloud twisting its way toward us.

"What's that?" I asked my mother as I ran through the door.

"A tornado! Get down in the basement!"

Mother made us all huddle together in the southwest corner of the basement. Frightened as I was, I could hear the wind blowing outside and heavy rain hitting the house. I could also hear a roar that sounded like a hundred airplanes flying overhead.

In a moment, the roar stopped and there was only the sound of the wind and rain.

When it was all over, we went back upstairs. The sun was beginning to shine. The temperature had dropped, and it was cool outside.

The tornado missed us. But it destroyed a house about a mile away, killing a woman and seriously injuring her two children.

It was just a small tornado, but still it did some terrible things.

Guess the meanings of words.

*Read each section of the story. Then read the statements that follow each section. Put **T** in front of each statement that is true. Put **F** in front of each statement that is false.*

All of a sudden, the sky turned yellow. I could hear my mother shouting to us to get into the house immediately. While running toward the house, I saw a dark, gray funnel-shaped cloud twisting its way toward us.

_____   1.   When people shout, they speak softly. They don't speak loudly.

_____   2.   *Immediately* means "later" or "in a few minutes."

Mother made us all huddle together in the southwest corner of the basement. Frightened as I was, I could hear the wind blowing outside and heavy rain hitting the house. I could also hear a roar that sounded like a hundred airplanes flying overhead.

_____   3.   When the children were *huddled together*, each child was in a different place in the basement.

_____   4.   *Frightened* means "afraid."

_____   5.   A *roar* is a soft noise.

_____   6.   *Overhead* means "above."

The tornado missed us. But it destroyed a house about a mile away, killing a woman and seriously injuring her two children.

It was just a small tornado, but still it did some terrible things.

_____   7.   The house was damaged.

_____   8.   *Terrible* means "good" or "wonderful."

Use words in context.

Write one word in each blank.

frightened   huddled   immediately   roar   shouted

Mother _____ to the children and told them to go to the basement _____. There the _____ children _____ together, listening to the wind, the rain, and a _____ that sounded like a hundred airplanes.

destroyed   injured   terrible

The tornado did some _____ things: It killed a woman, _____ two children, and _____ a house.

Check your comprehension.

*Read each section of the story. Then read the statements following each section. Put **T** in front of each statement that is true. Put **F** in front of each statement that is false.*

The summer day was very hot. I was just a child then and was playing outside with my friends.

In the late afternoon, dark clouds began to gather in the western sky, and later the wind began to blow. The clouds moved faster and faster toward us.

_____   1.   The weather suddenly became bad in the late afternoon.

_____   2.   The wind was very gentle.

All of a sudden, the sky turned yellow. I could hear my mother shouting to us to get into the house immediately. While running toward the house, I saw a dark, gray funnel-shaped cloud twisting its way toward us.

"What's that?" I asked my mother as I ran through the door.

"A tornado! Get down in the basement!"

_____   3.   Mother did not know that a tornado was coming.

_____   4.   The child saw the funnel-shaped cloud but did not know what it was.

Mother made us all huddle together in the southwest corner of the basement. Frightened as I was, I could hear the wind blowing outside and heavy rain hitting the house. I could also hear a roar that sounded like a hundred airplanes flying overhead.

———————— 5.   The child was afraid.

———————— 6.   The child was alone in the basement.

In a moment, the roar stopped and there was only the sound of the wind and rain.

When it was all over, we went back upstairs. The sun was beginning to shine. The temperature had dropped, and it was cool outside.

———————— 7.   The tornado lasted a long time.

———————— 8.   The weather was nice after the storm had passed.

The tornado missed us. But it destroyed a house about a mile away, killing a woman and seriously injuring her two children.

It was just a small tornado, but still it did some terrible things.

———————— 9.   The tornado did not destroy the child's house, but it did destroy another house about a mile away.

———————— 10.   The tornado killed three people.

Use information to make guesses.

Underline the words in the paragraph that tell you that the weather was changing.

In the late afternoon, dark clouds began to gather in the western sky, and later the wind began to blow. The clouds moved faster and faster toward us.

Underline the words in the paragraph that tell you it was very noisy in the basement.

Mother made us all huddle together in the southwest corner of the basement. Frightened as I was, I could hear the wind blowing outside and heavy rain hitting the house. I could also hear a roar that sounded like a hundred airplanes flying overhead.

Recall the story.

Try to tell (or write) the main ideas in the story. Use the following words and phrases as a guide.

hot summer afternoon	went back upstairs
weather changed suddenly	nice weather
mother shouted to the children	house destroyed
went to the basement	woman killed
rain, wind, roar	two children injured

Summarize the story.

Fill in the blanks with words from the reading.

One hot summer _____ a _____ came. Mother made us go down to the _____. We _____ together there. We heard a _____. In a few minutes, the _____ was gone. It _____ us, but it _____ another house nearby. It _____ two children and _____ their mother.

Talk about your experience.

Have you ever been in a severe storm? Tell your classmates about your experience.

Part Three — SEVERE WINDSTORMS

Listening

Listen for the main idea.

Your teacher will give you some information. Listen to the information. Then choose the answer which best tells what the information is about.

a. ways tropical cyclones and tornadoes are similar

b. reasons why tropical cyclones and tornadoes develop

c. ways in which tropical cyclones and tornadoes are similar and ways in which they are different

Listen for words.

Fill in the blanks while listening to the information again. Use the following words or expressions:

destroy property	storms
heavy rains	strong winds
kill people	tornadoes
severe windstorms	tropical areas
	tropical cyclones

_____ and _____ are similar in that they are both _____ with _____ and _____. Also, they both _____ and _____. The two _____ are different in that _____ are much bigger than _____. Also, _____ develop over water in _____, _____ develop over land.

Check your comprehension.

Your teacher will ask you some questions about the information. Listen to the questions. Then write out the answers to the questions.

1. a. _____.
   b. _____.

2. a. _____.
   b. _____.
   c. _____.

Listen to the information again. Check your answers while you listen.

Reading

Preview the reading.

Read the information quickly to find answers to the following questions.

1. What two kinds of severe windstorms does the reading discuss?

2. How many similarities does the reading mention?

3. Does the reading give an example of each kind of severe windstorm?

Severe Windstorms

Tornadoes and tropical cyclones are similar in that they both (1) are severe windstorms, (2) have circular winds that blow counterclockwise around an area of low pressure, (3) have strong winds and heavy rains, and (4) destroy property and kill people. They differ in a number of other ways, however.

Tropical cyclones are very large storms which develop over oceans. The winds blow at 80 miles per hour or more. Some tropical cyclones are more than 100 miles wide. Tropical cyclones cause flooding in coastal areas. Their winds blow down trees and damage buildings.

In 1900, a tropical cyclone (hurricane) with winds of 120 miles per hour hit Galveston, Texas. The storm caused the waters of the Gulf of Mexico to rise 15 feet above their normal level, and it produced waves that were 25 feet high. Galveston was destroyed by the high water and huge waves. More than 5,000 people drowned.

Tornadoes are smaller than tropical cyclones. They develop over land* during severe thunderstorms (rainstorms that have thunder and lightning). Most tornadoes are less than 110 yards wide, but their winds blow at 300 miles per hour or more. Tornadoes destroy almost everything that they touch.

Large tornadoes can kill many people. In March 1925, for example, a tornado killed 689 people as it traveled through three states in the United States. Two hundred thirty-four of those people lived in one town, Murphysboro, Illinois.

Guess the meanings of words.

Read the information. Then circle the letter in front of the answer that best defines the word.

Tornadoes and tropical cyclones are similar in that they both (1) are severe windstorms, (2) have circular winds that blow counterclockwise around an area of low pressure, (3) have strong winds and heavy rains, and (4) destroy property and kill people. They differ in a number of other ways, however.

1. Similar

   a. same
   b. different

2. Circular

   a. Circular winds blow in a straight line.
   b. Circular winds blow in a circle.

*Tornado-like windstorms that develop over water are called *waterspouts*.

3. Counterclockwise

   Counter means opposite or reverse. *Clockwise* means "in the same direction as a clock."

   a. Winds that blow counterclockwise turn in the same direction that the hands on a clock turn.
   b. Counterclockwise winds turn in the opposite direction that hands on a clock turn.

   Tropical cyclones are very large storms which develop over oceans. . . . Tropical cyclones cause flooding in coastal areas.

4. Coastal areas

   a. *Coastal areas* are places where the ocean meets land.
   b. *Coastal areas* are in the mountains away from the ocean.

   Tropical cyclones cause flooding in coastal areas. In 1900, a tropical cyclone (hurricane) with winds of 120 miles per hour hit Galveston, Texas. The storm caused the waters of the Gulf of Mexico to rise 15 feet above their normal level, and it produced waves that were 25 feet high. Galveston was destroyed by the high water and huge waves. More than 5,000 people drowned.

5. Flooding

   a. When there is flooding, everything is above water.
   b. When there is flooding, there is water everywhere.

6. Normal level

   a. The normal level of the water is the level (or height) it usually is every day.
   b. The normal level is the level the water is at during a storm.

7. Produce

   a. *Produce* means "make."
   b. *Produce* means "destroy."

8. Drown

   a. People drown when they are killed by high winds.
   b. People drown when they die in water.

Use words in context.

Write one word or expression in each blank.

circular   counterclockwise   similar   winds

The _____ of both tropical cyclones and tornadoes
are _____ in that they are _____ and
blow _____.

coastal flooding   normal level
drown   producing

Tropical cyclones make the sea rise above its _____,
_____ _____. As a result, people
sometimes _____.

Check your comprehension.

1. Which storm is larger, a tornado or a tropical cyclone?
   a. tropical cyclone
   b. tornado
   c. same size

2. Which storm has stronger winds?
   a. tropical cyclone
   b. tornado

3. Which storm has circular winds?
   a. tropical cyclone
   b. tornado
   c. both

4. During which storm does it rain?
   a. tropical cyclone
   b. tornado
   c. both

5. Which storm probably causes more damage to buildings?
   a. tropical cyclone
   b. tornado

Outline the reading.

Fill in the outline to show the similarities and differences of tropical cyclones and tornadoes.

I.   Similarities
    A. _____
    B. _____
    C. _____
    D. _____
II. Differences
    A. Tropical cyclones
       1. Develop _____
       2. Winds blow _____
       3. 100 miles _____
       4. Destruction
          a. flooding _____
          b. _____
          c. _____
          d. Example—storm that hit Galveston, Texas
    B. Tornadoes
       1. Develop _____
       2. Winds blow _____
       3. 110 yards _____
       4. Destroy _____
          a. Example—tornado that hit _____

Recall the reading.

Tell in which ways tropical cyclones and tornadoes are similar. Tell in which ways they are different.

Part Four

Outside Reading

Find more information about tornadoes and hurricanes.

1. *Look up* tornado *and* hurricane *in an encyclopedia. Look for one or two interesting facts about each that you have not learned in this lesson.*

2. *In an encyclopedia, look up one of the places listed in the chart. Try to find more information about a tropical cyclone that hit that place.*

Lesson 10

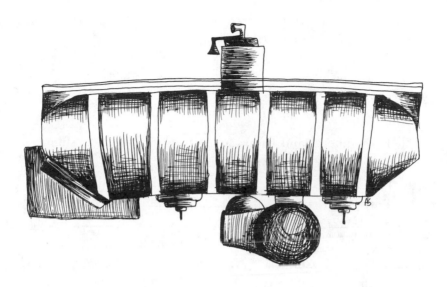

Part One — EXPLORING THE OCEANS

Listening

Listen for the main idea.

Your teacher is going to give you some information. Listen to the information. Then choose the sentence which best tells what the information is about.

a. The information tells about the oceans.

b. The information is about craft that explore the oceans.

c. The information discusses two ways to move along the bottom of the ocean.

Listen for words.

Fill in the blanks while listening to the information again. Use the following words or expressions:

attached	craft	spherical
bottom	explore	supplied
cables	motor	support ship

Bathyspheres and bathyscaphes were two kinds of submersible _____ that people used to _____ the ocean. These _____ went deep into the ocean.

Bathyspheres were _____ —round like a ball. They were _____ to a _____ by two _____. One cable pulled the _____ to the surface. The other cable _____ electricity and telephone.

Early bathyscaphes were also _____. They were not _____ by _____ to a _____. They had a _____ and could move along the _____ of the ocean.

Guess the meanings of words.

*Read the information. Then read the statements following the information. Put **T** in front of each statement that is true. Put **F** in front of each statement that is false.*

Bathyspheres and bathyscaphes were two kinds of submersible craft used by early explorers of the oceans. These submersible craft could go deep into the ocean. People rode in these underwater craft to go down to the bottom of the ocean. They descended into the water in order to explore the ocean bottom.

_____   1. Underwater craft went deep into the ocean.

_____   2. Underwater craft went under water.

_____   3. Bathyspheres and bathyscaphes were underwater craft.

_____   4. Bathyspheres and bathyscaphes could go under water.

_____   5. The bottom of the ocean is under water.

_____   6. *Descend* means to go up.

_____ 7. A submersible craft cannot go underwater.

_____ 8. *Go deep into the ocean* means go into the water only a little.

_____ 9. You learn about a place when you explore it.

_____ 10. An explorer is a person who explores.

The support ship, or mother ship, for a bathysphere is at the top, or surface, of the ocean. Two cables run from the support ship to the bathysphere. One cable pulls the bathysphere to the surface. The other cable supplies electricity and telephone.

_____ 11. The support ship is at the surface of the ocean.

_____ 12. The surface of the ocean is at the bottom of the ocean.

_____ 13. Cables run between the support ship and the bathysphere.

_____ 14. The cables are not important.

_____ 15. The mother ship pulls the bathysphere to the surface.

_____ 16. The bathysphere gets electricity and telephone from both cables.

_____ 17. *Supplies electricity and telephone* has about the same meaning as *brings electricity and telephone.*

_____ 18. The support ship and the mother ship are different ships.

Like a bathysphere, a bathyscaphe was also spherical (round like a ball). However, it was not attached to its support ship by cables. It had its own supply of electricity. Also, it had a motor so it could move along the bottom of the ocean.

_____ 19. A bathyscaphe was spherical, but a bathysphere was not spherical.

_____ 20. Something that is *spherical* is round like a ball.

_____ 21. Cables ran between the support ship and the bathyscaphe.

_____ 22. A bathysphere was attached to its support ship by cables.

_____ 23. When we say that a bathysphere was attached to its support ship by cables, we mean that cables went from the support ship to the bathysphere.

_____ 24. A bathyscaphe did not have its own supply of electricity.

_____ 25. A bathyscaphe used a motor to move along the bottom of the ocean.

_____ 26. *Move along the bottom* has almost the same meaning as *go along the bottom.*

Use words in context.

Write one word or expression in each blank.

bottom   craft   submersible

Bathyspheres and bathyscaphes were _____

_____ that went to the _____ of the

ocean.

craft   explored   spherical   underwater

Bathyspheres and bathyscaphes were _____

_____ that _____ the oceans. Both craft

were _____. That means they were round like a ball.

attached   cables   supplied   support ship

A bathysphere was _____ to its _____

by two _____. One of these cables _____

electricity and telephone.

bottom   motor   move along

A bathyscaphe could _____ the _____

because it had a _____.

Check your comprehension.

*Your teacher will ask you some questions about the information. Listen
to the questions. Then write out the answers to the questions.*

1. They were craft that could go deep _____.
2. People rode in them to _____.
3. _____.
4. _____.
5. _____.
6. _____.

Listen to the information again. Check your answers while you listen.

Reading

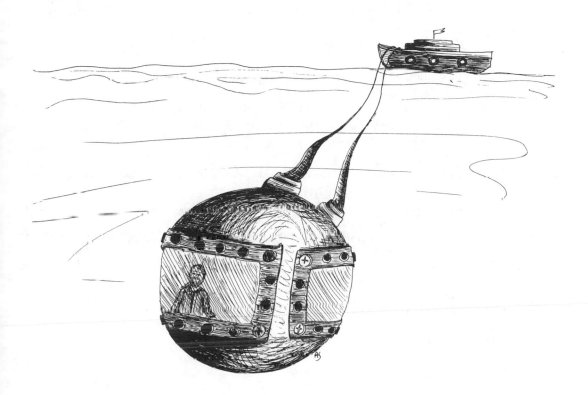

Preview the reading.

Quickly look through the introductory reading and the chart. Then answer the following questions.

1. What is the chart about?

2. Is the reading about the chart?

3. Does the reading discuss bathyspheres and bathyscaphes?

Submersible Craft

   The following chart is about submersible craft (underwater craft) that were used to explore oceans. The chart shows exploration dives made by bathyspheres and bathyscaphes from 1934 to 1960.

The bathyspheres were spherical, submersible craft. They were connected by two cables to their support ships. One cable was used to pull the craft to the surface. It was also used to pull the craft along the bottom when it was submerged. The other cable supplied electricity and telephone.

Bathyscaphes were also spherical. They were attached to the bottom of cigar-shaped tanks that were filled with gasoline. The gasoline, which was lighter than seawater, helped the craft float. Unlike bathyspheres, bathyscaphes were not connected to their support ships by cables. They descended and ascended on their own. Also, they had motors, so they could move horizontally to explore along the bottom.

EARLY DIVING CRAFT

YEAR	TYPE OF CRAFT*	IMPORTANT DIVE(S)	DIVER(S)	LOCATION
1934	Bathysphere	Manned dive to 3,028 ft.	William Beebe and his engineer	Bermuda
1946	Bathysphere (Benthoscope)	Manned dive to 4,488 ft.	Otis Barton	Santa Cruz, California
1946	Bathyscaphe (FNRS-2)	Manned test dive to 84 ft.	Auguste Piccard and Theodore Monod	Cape Verde
1946	Bathyscaphe (FNRS-2)	Unmanned dive to 4,544 ft.	————————	Cape Verde
1953	Bathyscaphe (FNRS-2)	Manned dive to 13,700 ft.	George Houot	Mediterranean Sea
1954	Bathyscaphe (Trieste)	Manned dive to 10,392 ft.	Name not available	Ponza, Italy
1959	Bathyscaphe (Trieste)	Manned dive to 18,105 ft.	Jacques Piccard and Andres Rechnitzer	Guam
1960	Bathyscaphe (Trieste)	Manned dive to 22,560 ft.	Jacques Piccard and Don Walsh	Guam
1960	Bathyscaphe (Trieste)	Manned dive to 35,800 ft.	Jacques Piccard and Don Walsh	Guam

*Names of craft are listed in parentheses.

Source: Compiled from *Manned Submersibles*. R. Frank Busby. Washington, D.C.: Office of the Oceanographer of the Navy, 1976, by permission of the U.S. Department of the Navy.

Guess the meanings of words.

*Read the information. Then read the statements following the informa-tion. Put **T** in front of each statement you think is true. Put **F** in front of each statement you think is false.*

A support ship floated on the surface of the water. A submersible craft dove to the bottom. When the support ship was at the bottom, it was submerged.

_____   1.   If something is floating, it is underwater.
_____   2.   Something that is floating is not submerged.
_____   3.   A submersible craft goes to the bottom.
_____   4.   A submersible craft is submerged when it is on the bottom.
_____   5.   Something that is underwater is submerged.
_____   6.   When something dives, it goes up out of the water.

A bathyscaphe was attached to the bottom of a tank that had the shape of a cigar.

_____   7.   The cigar-shaped tank looked like a cigar.
_____   8.   The bathyscaphe was above the tank.

A bathysphere was attached by cables to its support ship. One cable pulled the craft up when it ascended. The cable could also pull the bathysphere along the bottom while it was submerged.

_____   9.   Something goes down when it ascends.
_____ 10.   Something goes up when it ascends.

Use words in context.

Write one word in each blank.

> cigar-shaped   float

The _____ tank helped the bathyscaphe

_____.

> dives   submerged

A craft is _____ after it _____ to the bottom.

ascend   descended   pulled

The cable _____ the bathysphere along the bottom after it _____. It also pulled the craft up when it was time to _____.

Find specific information.

Answer the following questions quickly.

1. How many types of craft are listed in the chart?

2. Is the chart arranged according to year or according to depth of dive?

3. Which years are included in the chart?

4. In what year was the deepest dive? Who made that dive?

5. When was the shallowest dive? Who made that dive? (Note: *Shallow* is the opposite of *deep*.)

6. What did two men do in 1934?

Recall the information.

Describe a bathysphere in your own words (two or three sentences). Describe a bathyscaphe in your own words.

Give your opinion.

Which craft, a bathysphere or a bathyscaphe, was more dangerous? Why do you think so?

Part Two — THE SEA

Listening

Listen for the main idea.

Your teacher will give you some information. Listen to the information. Then choose the answer which best tells what the information is about.

a. strong storms and the sea
b. experiencing the sea
c. walking along beaches

Listen for words.

Fill in the blanks while listening to the information again. Use the following words or expressions:

beach	experienced	ocean depths	strong
blowing	explore	storm	waves
breeze			

People who _____ the _____ see
things that the rest of us never will. Still, most of us have _____
_____ the sea. Have you ever walked along a _____
on a cloudy winter day, or felt a cool, gentle _____
_____ in from the water after a hot summer day?
Or have you ever been on a ship during a _____
_____? Have you seen _____ so big
they could wash away houses and streets? Perhaps some of us have
_____ the ocean in a number of different ways.

Guess the meanings of words.

*Read the information. Then read the statements that follow the information. Put **T** in front of statements that are true. Put **F** in front of statements that are false.*

Submersible craft dive down to the ocean depths.

_____ 1. Ocean depths are at the surface of the ocean.
_____ 2. Ocean depths are deep places in the ocean.

A breeze is a gentle wind that comes off the ocean. It usually blows during early evening. A strong wind blows during a storm. Often, there are large waves during a storm.

_____ 3. A breeze is a strong wind.
_____ 4. A gentle wind is a strong wind.
_____ 5. There is a breeze during a storm.
_____ 6. A breeze is not a strong wind.
_____ 7. A strong wind blows hard. It is not gentle.
_____ 8. Waves are water.
_____ 9. Waves are wind.

Use words in context.

Write one word or expression in each blank.

blew	ocean depths	strong
breeze	storm	waves

The wind was too _____; the _____ were too large. The small ship broke up and sank to the _____. Then after the _____, a gentle _____ _____.

Check your comprehension.

Your teacher will ask you some questions about the information. Listen to the questions. Then write out the answers to the questions.

1. _____.
2. _____.
3. _____.

Listen to the information again. Check your answers while you listen.

Reading

Preview the reading.

The person who wrote this story was walking somewhere one day. Where was this person walking?

The Sea

These waves have rolled up on this beach thousands of years before me; they will be here thousands of years after I have died. Right now, these waves wash over my bare feet, and my toes sink into wet sand.

Sea gulls fly overhead this late afternoon while fishermen push their boats into the water and row out to sea. Tossed by waves, up and down, men in boats pull in nets, while housewives wait on shore to buy the fish the fishermen catch.

Tall pine trees—their roots in sandy soil—stand angled to the ground, having been bent landward by the strong winter winds.

I stroll along endlessly. I see a landmark down along the shore clearly, but it is so far. I walk and walk, but I never reach it. Finally, I turn around, for the evening sun is slipping down from the sky, sinking slowly into a red sea.

Clouds are aglow from the red sun, and in front of them the dark silhouette of a mountainous island appears.

Then with darkness, the sun, the sea, and the mountains all disappear. But the waves keep rolling in.

Guess the meanings of words.

*Read each section of the story. Then read the statements following each section. Put **T** in front of each statement that is true. Put **F** in front of each statement that is false.*

These waves have rolled up on this beach thousands of years before me; they will be here thousands of years after I have died. Right now, these waves wash over my bare feet, and my toes sink into wet sand.

_____ 1. Waves are coming up on the beach now.

_____ 2. Waves seldom come up on the beach.

_____ 3. The writer is wearing shoes.

_____ 4. *My toes sink into the wet sand* means my toes are going down into the wet sand.

_____ 5. *Thousands of years* means one or two thousand years.

Sea gulls fly overhead this late afternoon while fishermen push their boats into the water and row out to sea. Tossed by waves, up and down, men in boats pull in nets, while housewives wait on shore to buy the fish the fishermen catch.

_____ 6. The sea gulls are swimming.

_____ 7. *Overhead* means above the writer's head or up in the sky.

_____ 8. When fishermen *row out to sea*, they go out to sea in small boats.

_____ 9. Waves that toss boats up and down are small waves.

_____ 10. Fishermen use nets to catch fish.

Tall pine trees—their roots in sandy soil—stand angled to the ground, having been bent landward by the strong winter winds.

_____ 11. These pine trees are growing in sand.

_____ 12. When trees are *angled to the ground*, they are standing straight up and down.

_____ 13. *Landward* means in the direction of the ocean.

_____ 14. Strong winter winds are gentle winds.

I stroll along endlessly. I see a landmark down along the shore clearly, but it is so far. I walk and walk, but I never reach it. Finally, I turn around, for the evening sun is slipping down from the sky, sinking slowly into a red sea.

_____ 15. *Stroll* means "to walk." *Stroll along endlessly* means "to walk for a very long time."

_____ 16. The *landmark* is something the writer can see. Perhaps it is a building or a tree.

_____ 17. *Slipping down* has about the same meaning as *moving down*.

_____ 18. *Sinking* has about the same meaning as *moving down*.

Clouds are aglow from the red sun, and in front of them the dark silhouette of a mountainous island appears.

_____ 19. The clouds look like they are shining.

_____ 20. The writer can see only the shape of the island.

_____ 21. A mountainous island has no mountains.

_____ 22. A *silhouette . . . appears* means that the silhouette comes into view. The writer can now see it.

Use words in context.

Write one word or expression in each blank.

bare	roll up	sink	thousands of years

Her _____ feet _____ into the sand as she watches the waves _____ on shore—waves that have been rolling up for _____.

fly	nets	overhead	row	toss

Fishermen _____ boats out to sea, while sea gulls _____ _____. Then they _____ their _____ into the sea.

angled	bent	landward	rooted	strong

The trees, which are _____ in sand, stand _____ to the ground, having been _____ _____ by the _____ winter winds.

aglow	endlessly	mountainous	slipping
appears	landmark	silhouette	strolls

She _____ _____ toward a _____ which is far down the shore. Meanwhile, the red sun is slowly _____ into the sea; the clouds are _____, and a _____ of a _____ island _____ in front of them.

Determine the meanings of pronouns.

Write a noun in each blank. The noun must have the same meaning as the word just before the parentheses.

These waves have rolled up on this beach thousands of years before me; they (_____) will be here thousands of years after I am gone. Right now, these waves wash over my bare feet, and my toes sink into wet sand.

Sea gulls fly overhead this late afternoon while fishermen push their (_____) boats into the water and row out to sea. Tossed by waves, up and down, men in boats pull in nets, while housewives wait on shore to buy the fish the fishermen catch.

. . . I see a landmark down along the shore so clearly, but it (_____) is so far. I walk and walk, but I never reach it (_____).

. . . Clouds are aglow from the red sun, and in front of them (_____) the dark silhouette of a mountainous island appears.

Check your comprehension.

*Read each section of the story. Then read the statements which follow each section. Put **T** in front of each statement that is true. Put **F** in front of each statement that is false.*

These waves have rolled up on this beach thousands of years before me; they will be here thousands of years after I have died. Right now, these waves wash over my bare feet, and my toes sink into wet sand.

_____ 1. The writer is looking at the ocean.

_____ 2. The writer is thinking that the ocean has been there since the beginning of time.

_____ 3. The writer is thinking that the ocean will go away when she dies.

_____ 4. The writer's feet are wet.

Sea gulls fly overhead this late afternoon while fishermen push their boats into the water and row out to sea. Tossed by waves, up and down, men in boats pull in nets, while housewives wait on shore to buy the fish the fishermen catch.

_____ 5. The writer is describing what she sees.

_____ 6. It is early in the morning.

_____ 7. The people waiting on shore will probably cook fish for dinner tonight.

_____ 8. The fishermen have already returned to shore with their catch of fish.

Tall pine trees—their roots in sandy soil—stand angled to the ground, having been bent landward by the strong winter winds.

_____ 9. The trees stand angled to the ground because of the fierce winter winds.

I stroll along endlessly. I see a landmark down along the shore clearly, but it is so far. I walk and walk, but I never reach it. Finally, I turn around, for the evening sun is slipping down from the sky, sinking slowly into a red sea.

_____ 10. The writer is taking a short walk along the beach.
_____ 11. The writer walks as far as the landmark.
_____ 12. The writer decides to go back because it is getting dark.

Clouds are aglow from the red sun, and in front of them the dark silhouette of a mountainous island appears.

_____ 13. The clouds have turned bright red.
_____ 14. The sun is setting behind the mountain.

Then with darkness, the sun, the sea, and the mountains all disappear. But the waves keep rolling in.

_____ 15. It is now night.
_____ 16. The writer can still see the sun, the sea, and the mountains.
_____ 17. There are no longer any waves.

Use information to make guesses.

Put **T** in front of statements you think are true; put **F** in front of statements you think are false.

_____ 1. The writer enjoyed the walk along the sea.
_____ 2. The writer is saying that people are on earth just a short time.
_____ 3. The writer didn't think that the sunset was beautiful.

Recall the story.

Write or tell as much of the story as you can remember. Do not look back at the story. Tell where the writer was walking, what the writer saw, and what the writer was thinking.

Talk about a hike.

Tell (or write) about a walk or a hike that you enjoyed a lot.

Part Three — SUBMERSIBLE CRAFT

Listening

Listen for the main idea.

Your teacher will give you some information. Listen to the information. Then choose the sentence which best tells what the information is about.

a. Engineers can easily design submersible craft.

b. It is difficult for engineers to design submersible craft.

c. Engineers need to consider depth and lighting when they design submersible craft.

Listen for words.

Fill in the blanks while listening to the information again. Use the following words or expressions:

artificial	depth	pressure
consider	design	resist
deep	lighting	

Use additional blanks.

Engineers need to _____ _____ and _____ _____ when they _____ a submersible craft. They need to _____ _____ because water _____ _____ in the ocean is very great. The submersible must be able to _____ strong water

_____. Engineers need to _____
_____ _____ because the deep ocean is
very dark. The craft must have _____ lights so that the
people in the craft can see where they are going and what they are doing.

Guess the meanings of words.

Read the information. Then circle the letter in front of the answer that best defines the word.

Engineers need to consider many things when they design a new submersible craft.

1. Consider
   a. Engineers need to think about many things.
   b. Engineers do not have to think about many things.

2. Design
   a. They consider many things after the craft is built and goes under water.
   b. They consider many things when they make plans for a new submersible craft.

Water pressure increases with depth. As a craft descends deeper into the ocean, water pressure increases greatly. For example, at a depth of 10 feet water pressure is 65 pounds per square inch. At 6,000 feet the pressure is more than 2,600 pounds per square inch.

3. Depth
   a. If a craft is 1,000 feet deep in the ocean, it is at a depth of 1,000 feet.
   b. If a craft is 2,000 feet deep in the ocean, it is at a depth of 100 feet.

4. Water pressure
   a. Water pressure is the pressure or force of water against the surface of the craft.
   b. Water pressure is the depth of the water.

A submersible must be strong enough to resist great water pressure. It must not fall apart or be damaged when it descends to depths where the water pressure is great.

5. Resist
   a. The submersible must not descend to depths where the water pressure is great.
   b. The submersible must be able to "fight off" water pressure.

Sunlight does not travel far into the ocean. Therefore, a craft must have artificial lights.

6. Artificial light
   a. Artificial light is sunlight.
   b. Artificial light is made by people.

Use words in context.

Write one word in each blank.

artificial	depth	pressure (2)
consider	design	resist
deep	lighting	

Engineers must _____ _____ and _____ when they _____ submersible craft. A craft must be able to _____ _____ in _____ water, and it must have _____ lights.

Check your comprehension.

Your teacher will ask you some questions about the information. Listen to the questions. Then write out the answers to the questions.

1. _____.
2. a. _____.
   b. _____.

Listen to the information again. Check your answers while you listen.

Reading

Preview the reading.

Look at the headings in the readings. List five problems engineers must consider.

1. _____   4. _____
2. _____   5. _____
3. _____

Designing Submersible Craft

When engineers design submersible craft to explore the oceans, they must consider several problems.

Pressure

First, engineers must consider water pressure. A submersible craft that dives deep into the ocean must be able to withstand a great amount of water pressure. The deeper a submersible goes, the more water pressure it must resist. For example, at a depth of 10 feet, water pressure is about 65 pounds per square inch (psi); at 100 feet, it is about 652 psi; and at 6,000 feet, it is 2,674.8 psi.

Since water pressure increases with depth, engineers must first determine the depth at which the submersible will operate. Then they can design the vehicle to operate safely at that depth.

Temperature

Second, engineers must consider temperature. The submersible must be able to withstand extremes of temperature. It must not crack, for example, when it goes into cold water. Also, temperatures inside the submersible must remain comfortable even when the temperature of the water changes.

Density

Third, engineers must consider density. The density (thickness) of the water affects the buoyancy (ability to float in water) of a submersible. Seawater density varies with depth, temperature, and salinity (amount of salt). Engineers must be certain that the submersible will have the proper buoyancy.

Light

Fourth, engineers must equip submersibles with proper lighting. Divers in submersibles must have artificial light to see, because at depths lower than 1,000 there is not enough sunlight to see things in detail.

Acoustics

Finally, engineers have to consider how sound travels through water. Sound travels faster in warm water near the surface than it does in deeper, cooler water. Therefore, there may sometimes be refraction (bending of the sound waves). This refraction limits the distance over which a support ship and its submersible can maintain voice contact.

Source: Adapted from *Manned Submersibles*. R. Frank Busby. Washington, D.C.: Office of the Oceanographer of the Navy, 1976. Used by permission of the U.S. Department of the Navy.

Guess the meanings of words.

*Read the information. Then read the statements following the information. Put **T** in front of statements that are true. Put **F** in front of statements that are false.*

A submersible craft that dives deep into the ocean must be able to withstand a great amount of water pressure. The deeper a submersible goes, the more water pressure it must resist.

_____ 1. *Resist* and *withstand* have about the same meaning here.

_____ 2. *Withstand* means "to dive deep into the ocean."

The submersible must be able to withstand extremes of temperature. It must not crack, for example, when it goes into cold water. Also, temperatures inside the submersible must remain comfortable even when the temperature of the water changes.

_____ 3. A change from warm to cool is an extreme temperature change.

_____ 4. A change from very hot to very cold is an extreme temperature change.

_____ 5. *Crack* and *break* have similar meanings.

_____ 6. Water might enter a submersible if it cracks.

_____ 7. We feel bad when temperatures are uncomfortable.

The density (thickness) of the water affects the buoyancy (ability to float in water) of a submersible. Seawater density varies with depth, temperature, and salinity (amount of salt).

_____ 8. Something that is dense is not thick.

_____ 9. A rock has good buoyancy.

_____ 10. Fresh water is saline.

Engineers must equip submersibles with proper lighting. Divers in submersibles must have artificial light to see, because at depths lower than 1,000 feet there is not enough sunlight to see things in detail.

_____ 11. *Proper* means "the wrong kind."

_____ 12. *Equip* and *give* have similar meanings.

Refraction limits the distance over which a support ship and its submersible can maintain voice contact.

_____ 13. The people in the submersible and the people on the support ship can talk to each other if they have voice contact.

_____ 14. To *maintain voice contact* means to stop being able to talk with someone.

_____ 15. Because the distance over which voice contact can be maintained is limited, a submersible will lose voice contact if it goes too far from the support ship.

Use words in context.

Write one word in each blank.

comfortable   cracking   extremes   resist

A submersible must _____ _____ even if it experiences _____ of temperature. The inside of the craft must also remain _____.

equipped   proper

A submersible must be _____ with _____ lights.

limits   maintain

Refraction _____ the distance over which a support ship and its submersible can _____ voice contact.

buoyancy   density   salinity

The _____ of seawater varies with depth, temperature, and _____. _____ is affected by density.

Find specific information.

Write out answers to the following questions.

1. List five problems engineers encounter when they design submersible craft.

   a. _____   d. _____

   b. _____   e. _____

   c. _____

2. Why must engineers consider pressure?

3. What does *psi* mean?

4. Why must engineers consider temperature?

5. Why must engineers consider density?

6. What is buoyancy?

7. Why must engineers think about light?

8. Why must engineers consider acoustics?

9. What is refraction?

Summarize the reading.

Write a short paragraph which summarizes the reading. Use the following questions as a guide.

1. What are five things engineers must consider when they design submersible craft?

2. Why must they consider each of those five things?

Discuss design considerations.

Suppose you were designing a spacecraft to travel to the moon. What are some things you would have to take into consideration?

Part Four

Outside Reading

Learn about engineers.

What are some different kinds of engineers? Look up engineer *in an encyclopedia. Find out what different kinds of engineers are called.*

Learn about scuba diving.

Look up scuba diving *in an encyclopedia. Find out one difference between scuba diving and diving in submersible craft.*